A MEMOIR

we   already

have   a woman

we   like.

my life in the CIA

Lucy Kirk

Dectora Press
New York, NY
USA

Pring ISBN: 979-8-35094-812-7
eBook ISBN: 979-8-35094-813-4

DEDICATED TO

the girls that were

and the women to come

TABLE OF CONTENTS

AUTHOR'S NOTE

As a retired CIA employee, I am obligated to present any writing I do relating to my career to the Prepublication Classification Review Board (PCRB) in CIA Headquarters so that they may review and determine whether there is anything in my writing that is classified or too revealing in terms of my career. That said, you will see deletion markings in black throughout the book. Sometimes these markings result in incomplete sentences. It is my hope that you can read the material and get the gist of what I am saying throughout without the deleted words. I have done the best I can to keep the flow of my writing going. Places I served and lengths of time are notably absent per PCRB guidelines, and I have no specific words to fill in those parts.

ONCE UPON A TIME . . .

The year the Class of 1962 entered Wellesley College, the *Harvard Crimson* published a satirical article entitled "Tunicata." The editorial was about Wellesley women, a welcome-to-college to the freshman class. It described "Wellesley girls" as people who get married right after graduation, reproduce, and then drop to the bottom of the sea, never to be heard from again—like tunicata, the sea squirt.

"The tunicata are thin, lithe animals that move about the sea in their youth, investigating their surroundings. Then one day they grow fat, settle down on the ocean floor—never to move again—and reproduce."

The editorial made a powerful impression on this particular freshman class, which was made up of females who would enter adulthood amid the birth of feminism, the pill, and the 1960s. "Tunicata" somehow symbolized the message and character of what we were then. It revealed our hopes and dreams while also containing the cynicism and language to inspire and motivate many of us to push the boundaries. The mission of our generation of females held some promise, but there was no clarity. Nearly every career beyond marriage and "old maidism" had yet to be identified, much less attained.

CHAPTER ONE

THE TIMES— THE BEGINNING OF AN ERA

One evening, one of my college friends was coming home from a date with her boyfriend, a Harvard student and fledgling poet. She described the events of the evening, excitedly referring to vivid colors and heightened awareness. At first we thought she was enamored of the fellow, but we soon realized that she only spoke of bright colors and vivid images, not specifically of him. At the time, I wondered what she had been drinking, but I was not aware of alcohol producing this kind of euphoric state. Invariably I would be the one to take the phone messages from her swain, who always left them in poetry or verse form. I soon learned that she was sitting in on an experimental group run by a Harvard professor, one Timothy Leary. They were trying out a mushroom plant called psilocybin, and the results were being observed and studied by the professor.

It was the beginning of an era, but who knew that then? It was only later, and well after she had stopped dating the erstwhile poet, that Timothy Leary was asked to leave Harvard, from whence he began a remarkable career of his own as the father of the

about-to-be-born drug culture of America, and one of the defini-
tive players of the sixties and the entire society that emerged out of
that era.

The young man I dated at the time was an MIT student who
liked to frequent the Mt. Auburn Street Cafe in Cambridge, because
he had a crush on its resident singer. The singer was pretty and had
long black hair and a stunning soprano voice. Her name was Joan
Baez. My boyfriend was not the only one who would notice her. She
soon went on to make her own mark on our generation. The times
were being defined.

Fidel Castro spoke at Harvard, and many of us had heard him
but didn't know what to make of his political emergence. Several
friends of mine described their excitement hearing this dynamic
speaker and his hopeful message. Communism was just coming to
the Western Hemisphere—and its Soviet influences and threats to
U.S. national security interests were only beginning to gain attention
outside of Washington and Western security centers.

During my last two years at Wellesley, I began studying Spanish
in earnest. One evening in April 1961, I was sitting in a dormmate's
room listening to the radio, which carried shortwave Spanish language broadcasts. It was one of the few venues where I could actually
hear Spanish and practice my interpretational skills. As I listened
that evening, I translated a repeating message about a fish, a rainbow, and a tree. I simply could not make sense of the words, but
the message continued to be repeated, and I was certain that I was
translating it accurately. I finally went to bed, somewhat discouraged
at my lack of progress in learning Spanish.

Years later, when I was well into my career, I learned that my
translation had been correct after all. The message was indeed about

a fish, a rainbow, and a tree. It was part of the radio message that was being communicated by anti-Castro elements from Swan Island in the Caribbean, in essence the call to arms for the Bay of Pigs invasion of April 1961.

When I graduated in 1962, I had a plan. I would get married, have three or four children, and "do something different." Yes, that was my career aim—to do "something different." The Wellesley Placement Office didn't help much with my finding employment in any sector. They politely made it clear that there were very few professional jobs for young female graduates. The Help Wanted ads in local newspapers were my only means of finding a job. I had minimal counseling, but was told that I would have to learn to type if I were to get any kind of reasonable job. I had made it through my four years of college having friends type my papers for me at twenty-five cents a page. It had never occurred to me that I would need to learn to type on my own.

I headed off to Argentina that summer with the Experiment in International Living. Everyone thought I should go to France, but I said, "No, I'll be living in Paris one day. I need something more exotic." At the time, Argentina was that—exotic. The whole experience did expand my worldview. I was being drawn into the international life. I fell in love with the family I lived with in Buenos Aires, and with Argentina and the Latin world. I now added "international" to my very short list of job requirements.

Back from Argentina in my home town, Columbus, Ohio, I headed to the Columbus Business University (CBU) with a cousin to learn typing and speedwriting. It was not the Harvard Business

School—the first woman had just been admitted there, and it wasn't me. I was going to typing school. At the end of the three-months at CBU, I said a sad goodbye to my family and headed back East. My classmates who didn't immediately get married and start families were also taking jobs as secretaries or primary school teachers. A few had ventured to New York to work in publishing houses or art galleries or museums, but those few had "New York" connections. I joined five other college friends in a two-bedroom house on the outskirts of Cambridge. The six of us were starting adult life together, dating a range of young men from the Boston area. It all seemed good enough.

But now I had to get a job. While in Argentina and at CBU, I had kept in contact with the Wellesley Placement Office, and in short order, I found a lead that promised to address some of my professional interests and help me determine what path I might take if I were to work for more than a couple of years. There was an opening with a microbiologist physician at the esteemed Peter Bent Brigham Hospital, where I could earn a salary of sixty-five dollars a week working as his secretary.

I got the job and was excited about it, since my father was a surgeon and I had given some thought to the idea of becoming a doctor myself. I saw my father as brilliantly successful and as helping other humans in their times of suffering—an ideal combination. Unfortunately I didn't have a premed background. In fact I had no medical background at all and minimal scientific training. At the time, that was not part of the Wellesley curriculum. My early forays into zoology during my freshman year had not been entirely satisfying. Studying the body of a lobster and the genetics of the fruit fly did not inspire me to go on to the study of more complicated anatomical systems. Still, while at the Brigham, I had the chance to rethink the medical option and to consider whether I should devote at least four years to premed and medical school, even though such a rigorous academic course would not allow me time to pursue my personal plans, which included marriage and starting a family of my own.

It was perhaps a godsend that my office at the Brigham was right next to the Pathology Department. One afternoon while at my desk, I looked up to observe two orderlies carrying a large wrapped object by my door.

"What is that?" I asked one of the orderlies, somewhat aggressively.

"It's a leg," he responded. They were delivering it to the pathology lab.

I sat back down at my desk, my stomach lurching, and started rethinking my plan to go into medicine. My goal was to save lives, but I'd given little thought to the necessity of dealing with the physical bodies involved. Reality was beginning to sink into my medical dreams. I began to lose some of my enthusiasm for that line of work, particularly when I thought about what I would have to do to cadavers.

I was not going to be a doctor, so I turned to the only other thing that had gained my attention in this short period of time—international work. The trip to Argentina had broadened my focus, but I had no idea how to narrow it down into something workable. I had no advisers on my new area of interest among my peers or family. So I would have to develop my "something" on my own and without any role model.

I soon found a job working for the assistant dean at the Fletcher School of Law and Diplomacy at Tufts University, where my salary increased a few dollars over my weekly Brigham pay. Money wasn't a problem, as I was sharing rent with my five classmates. I wasn't particularly interested in money anyway. No Wellesley girl was. My sense of the future and my entire planning package consisted of this: something would surely happen to me (I didn't know what) and I would marry a responsible, success-oriented man who would be madly in love with me, and we'd have children. The rest would take care of itself.

After a year working at Fletcher, my boss took me under his wing. His wife was a Wellesley grad as well, and he wanted me to head down a more productive path than I was clearly on. He urged me to consider attending graduate school. He knew that I was interested in international relations and encouraged me to take my interest to a deeper level. He was the first person who had actually shown a career interest in me, and one of the few whom I would meet along the way for many years to come. I was grateful to him for his advice, as by now I'd realized that I had to do something more fulfilling than flit from job to job while awaiting marriage or some other magnificent destiny. I would go to graduate school.

I was able to delay my career plans and take another detour into the academic world. I applied to and was accepted at the American University's School of International Service in Washington, D.C. But before that, I ventured off to Europe, East Germany, and Egypt for a summer with friends, then I headed to Washington, for graduate school. It was one of the few graduate schools where I could take Latin American Area Studies.

The Kennedy presidency ushered in an era of particular idealism for many Americans, especially young Americans who wanted to see a better world. Working for the U.S. government or doing service to the country, beyond the military, were appealing once again. *Non Ministrari sed Ministrare,* "not to be ministered unto, but to minister," the Wellesley motto, fit in well with the high aims espoused and supported by the country's leadership at the time— from the civil rights movement and the call to end racism, to the Peace Corps, the Alliance for Progress with Latin America, and their stated intention to end the nuclear arms race and implement a comprehensive nuclear test ban. We were soon to witness with horror the assassination of President John F. Kennedy, but many of us had chosen or would soon choose careers that were service or country oriented. Whatever truths have been uncovered since, the Kennedy era was a time of high ideals and expectations for our country and for many of us as individuals. Though marked by an overarching sadness because of the tragic assassination of the president, it was an inspiring time to be in Washington, a time when a career in government was viewed with honor and with hope for change.

I was now back in school, at the School of International Service and the consortium of Washington D.C. universities involved in international relations educational programs. By the time I was twenty-seven, I had a master's degree in Latin American Area Studies, a BA in liberal arts from one of the Seven Sisters, and my business degree in typing and speedwriting.

CHAPTER TWO

WASHINGTON, D.C.

It was once again time to find a job, but this time a serious one, one with a future. So I set off in the scorching heat of a Washington summer to do so. Now I knew I wanted "something international," and I decided to apply for every job in Washington that had the word *international* in its name, its program, anything. A couple of male graduate school friends of mine suggested I apply to the Central Intelligence Agency. The Agency was a mere twenty years old at the time, and I not much more. The CIA, I thought, that strange organization that deals with UFOs! That's all I had ever heard about the CIA in the mid-sixties, except that the guys recommending I apply said the CIA was secretly hiding little green bodies—presumably deceased—which they kept in a secure and secret facility somewhere in Ohio. They said the U.S. government was studying these aliens in addition to other nondomestic activities, whatever that meant.

I wasn't daunted by the little green bodies, and with some research and help from my graduate school adviser, I found a CIA personnel office on 16th Street, N.W. in downtown Washington. I made the appointment and in the dogged heat headed there for the interview.

A well-dressed gentleman of a certain age opened the door to a drab, minimally decorated office. I gave him my résumé and waited for his response. It was more than I had hoped for. He soon told me that, if accepted, I would have a variety of career opportunities involving international work. Good so far. And it would begin with my participating in a training program that would open broad opportunities—and the chance for international travel. More school and the chance to travel abroad! Enticing words to me. My "something different" was beginning to take shape. He went on to say that some of those opportunities included international affairs, finance, economics, the sciences, personnel, and administration. The potential seemed infinite. I could do almost anything if I joined the CIA, and I could do it overseas.

I was hooked and hadn't heard anything about little green bodies or other esoterica that might have dissuaded me from moving forward. I went back to the house in Georgetown that I was sharing with two college friends and decided to take another look at my résumé with an eye toward expanding it. The next day, I took it to the 16th Street office.

No one was there. The office appeared to have been evacuated. What was this place and where had the office moved? I didn't know anything about safe houses or disappearing offices at the time, and perhaps I just happened to return to the interview site the day this particular personnel office moved. It was nonetheless a strange beginning to what would ultimately become my career. I mailed my improved résumé to the general address I already had and waited.

I soon learned that they were "interested" in me as well, but I was advised that I would have to wait for the clearance process on me to be completed. Researching my entire background, clean as it was, could take up to six months. I took a temporary job at the Library of

Congress, where I could again live in a quasi-academic atmosphere. My breaks consisted of either chatting with the charming and flirtatious East European men—all married—who worked in the research part of the library, or wandering among the vast array of books, where fascinating, historic ones were shelved, along with some old copies of movie star magazines. I spent my spare time looking at the movie magazines and rare books on the Spanish conquest of Latin America, on which I was writing a grad school paper.

As the months passed, I became increasingly enthusiastic about working for the CIA. It was now the only thing I wanted to do. In the meantime, and to keep my options open, I interviewed with another government agency, one that also required clearances, but the procedures in this case moved very quickly and I was promptly in the "security" interview. The stern and starchy security officer who questioned me started our session by asking if I had anything I wished to "report." He did not use the word "confess." It was a strange question, one I had never encountered even with my parents. I was somewhat embarrassed at the very little that had happened in my life thus far, and my absence of sins to tell him about. I perhaps blushed and admitted that I might have a few unpaid parking tickets. The security officer frowned and promptly told me that this could be a matter of concern. My apparent blushing and bemused look led him to believe that I had not taken the offenses seriously. I left the interview chastened and now worried about the status of my CIA clearance reviews. Perhaps this was why the process was taking so long. I was not as sinless as I thought.

CHAPTER THREE

SIGNING ON

Six months after my initial CIA interview, I was notified that I had been accepted into the CIA's Career Training (CT) Program. I knew nothing about being a CT, but it sounded as if they had taken my application seriously and elevated me to a higher level of entry than I had anticipated. I was told that this was the "special" professional training course for intelligence officers, comparable to the Foreign Service at the Department of State, and that it would give me the information and background I needed to prepare for my career track, even though I didn't exactly sense at the time that I was embarking on a long-term career.

The training course began in the summer, but by this time, April 1967, I had become so eager to join that I wanted to "Enter on Duty" (EOD) right away and not wait until the course began in July. They arranged for me to do that and put me in an interim assignment.

On my first workday, I drove from Georgetown over the Key Bridge and made my way out to Langley, Virginia, where I looked for the old Bureau of Roads and Mines sign that marked the entrance to CIA Headquarters. It was a beautiful drive along the George

Washington Parkway, which in those days was pretty much countryside. I located the sign and CIA Headquarters. With proper identification and a statement that I was a new employee, I entered the grounds and found West Parking Lot, the farthest out lot, where all newcomers parked. West was one of the first locales any new CIA employee learned about. Parking there immediately identified you as a new and low-level employee, but it was an inviting site to me on that first day.

Excited at what lay ahead, I made my way into the main building, where I was photographed and given a temporary badge. There was and is no way past the security guards and into CIA Headquarters without a badge. The guards sent me directly to the Badge Office, where I was soon provided with the permanent badge and a chain, which I was to wear around my neck at all times while in the CIA.

I don't recall much about the signing-in ceremony except that it entailed a Secrecy Agreement. I had of course understood that I would be doing classified work if I joined the Agency, but now I actually put my name to a document promising that I would not discuss my work, my affiliation, the exact locations of offices, my colleagues, and of course any classified information—not ever, even with anyone in my immediate family. I certainly didn't expect to discuss classified work, but the totality of my commitment to no discussion was significant.

Since I had not originally been advised of the extent of the classified agreement, I had already told my family and two roommates that I was applying for work at the Agency. I was now to begin the more delicate business of trying to explain to others where I went every day. It was tricky, since I purportedly worked at the Pentagon—my cover position—not in Langley, Virginia. The first challenge would be to fend off friends who wanted to meet me for lunch some place near my purported office.

After being sworn in, I was taken to the personnel office of the DDP, the Deputy Director for Plans, later known as the Directorate of Operations (the DO). The DDP, or the Clandestine Service, was the operational arm of the Agency, and the one for which I unequivocally wanted to work. Although I knew almost nothing about the entire organization, I had read about the DDP and received some information on it in my initial interviews. To me it seemed the core of the organization—the center of all the international activity, travel, and intrigue. In later years, I would wonder about my early choices and overall career progress, that perhaps I would have done better in the analytical side of the organization, the Directorate of Intelligence (DI), but in the beginning, I had no doubt that I wanted to be in the DO.

In short order, I was assigned on a temporary duty basis (TDY) to the Latin American Division of the DO. Based on my background, it was the logical place for me to be assigned, the region where I had some language capabilities and substantive knowledge.

I was immediately sent to a desk in the Central American section, where I was given the portfolio to follow certain guerrilla activity in one of the small Central American countries. I reported to a woman just two years older than I, who was not a CT herself. She seemed very capable, though I soon noticed that she and a few colleagues had only pejorative comments to make about the CTs. I was beginning to understand that the training course was indeed special, and that, as a female, I was lucky to be in it. This did not start me off on the right foot with every other colleague, since the immediate perception was that I might get special treatment.

I had just completed my final graduate school paper, which covered Latin American reaction to the U.S. invasion of the Dominican Republic in 1965. I had spent months at the Organization of American States (OAS) and at the Library of Congress doing research. Spanish-language newspapers were nearly the only sources for my paper, which was critical of U.S. policy. While working on it, I developed great admiration for Senator William Fulbright, who strongly opposed the invasion.

As fate would have it, in my new assignment I worked for the senior officer who had been in charge of the intelligence portion of the Dominican Republic invasion. I asked him about the incident, explaining that I had just completed my graduate paper on it. He then outlined to me the justification for the invasion, describing the dangers of the previous Dominican leadership.

I had been well aware of opposing views on the invasion, but to date, I had certainly not had access to covert sources. Now I had a chance to discuss the action firsthand and broaden my perspective. While it was no surprise that I had been drawing conclusions only from publicly available material, I saw for the first time the critical role that intelligence could and did play in the formulation of U.S. foreign policy. It was not that my philosophical position changed, but that I began to see there was much more to the story than was available anywhere in the public domain, even to U.S. senators in the days before congressional oversight. I cannot say how many times over the years I've wished that more information could be available to the public on key international issues. Specific criticisms aside, I became a true believer in the role of intelligence and the commitment to its integrity.

In the meantime, I was learning my new job. The substantive part was quite straightforward and easy for me, but initially the security considerations boggled the mind. My female colleague was very helpful in getting me started, explaining the complex procedures used in writing any material of a classified nature. It was a daunting prospect to learn the administrative aspect of the job, since I had rarely even opened a safe, much less filed every single piece of paper I wrote or saw in one. I certainly didn't know what a "burn bag" was, nor had I developed the practice of shredding everything I wrote or read.

I was given my own burn bag, a brown sack marked SECRET, and told to put all my used classified materials in it. Once the bag was filled, I was to walk down to a central corridor and dump it into a wall slot designed for the receipt of burn bags. Like every other newcomer, I was told that I should yell my badge number and a warning, such as, "Watch out below. Burn bag coming," when I threw my full bag down the chute. We were told that for security reasons we should never yell our name, just our badge number. This particular piece of guidance was something of an initiation rite in the DO, a little game that was played on all the newcomers. I did what I was told and yelled down the chute on that first occasion, only to notice that several people were looking at me with smiles on their faces. It was clear that I was the new person on the block. In the future, I threw many bags of shredded material away, but never again yelled my badge number and a warning as I did so.

I began to develop some friends among my colleagues. Most were more than willing to be helpful and give advice to an absolute newcomer. One colleague in particular visited me with some consistency. He was smart, had traveled extensively, and was a great mentor in my new job. Though he was not yet even middle aged, I learned that he was already on his third marriage. I hadn't seen much of that in my life so far either. I didn't particularly notice his flirtatious side, and I had no thought of dating a colleague anyway, much less someone who was married.

So it was odd to me when, after I'd been on the desk for a few weeks, my female colleague said she wanted to warn me about this particular man, who seemed to be a friend of hers. She suggested that he was something of a playboy and shouldn't really be hanging around our office.

Then, the chief of the department, the very same man I had grown to admire because of his broad experience with the Dominican Republic, called me in for a little review. He directly stated to me that if I wanted "to have an affair," I should do it on my own time. I was horrified. I had never had an affair with anyone, and I certainly had no intention of beginning then and there, and with a married man. I don't even remember what I answered, as it was the first time in my life that I had ever had such a conversation and I was speechless. It seemed ridiculous to me, but I was nonetheless embarrassed that anyone, much less my senior manager, would see me in this light.

I left the room abashed. My male colleague came around the next day, and I virtually screeched to him in a loud whisper that I could no longer talk with him. He was taken aback, both at my remarks and my appalling behavior. He asked what was wrong, and I said I could not be seen with him. He then urged me to explain myself. I caved in and said I would meet him in the stairwell in ten minutes. We met, and he promptly warned me that meeting in the stairwell made it appear we had something to hide. I explained my dilemma to him and told him that I didn't want him to come to my office anymore. I don't even know if I was polite, since I was still alarmed at what my boss had said the day before. Though my friend suggested that I was drawing attention to us and that I was not being very cool, to say the least, I repeated that I could no longer talk to him.

I didn't take this event as a warning or even a symptom of some of the things that were to come. I just saw it as embarrassing and totally inappropriate as it related to me. In retrospect, it was my first DO setback as "a female". At the time I didn't have any idea there was discrimination against women. I had never given the subject much thought since I had not been particularly exposed to it anywhere in my education or upbringing.

My three-month interim ended and, before I knew it, I was sitting among a group of some one hundred fellow CTs at a building known as Blue University, "The Blue U." Since we were alphabetical, I was destined to make friends initially among the H–M group in the alphabet. There was no time to mix with anyone else.

The course was like a fast-moving trip abroad. For those of us who were totally new to every aspect of intelligence work, it was a complete learning experience. One day we were studying factory markings, which was the business of identifying certain military equipment by serial number; the next day map reading; then country analysis; and finally the history of the top Communist regimes. The crash course in maps covered every imaginable aspect of maps and made me realize how little I knew about this common subject, but I learned a lot and it has been useful ever since. We had to type all our written work. Fortunately, I had my degree from the Columbus Business University, so I wasn't a beginner at typing.

The people who seemed to excel in the course were the handful of men who had already been working in the Agency and who were taken into the CT course because they showed special promise based on their work to date. For one thing, they knew how to handle safes. I spent excessive amounts of time opening and closing my safe, neither step of which I ever got right on the first try. The insiders also understood the formats and procedures used—every project and every office required a certain kind of paperwork, which in turn called for its own special classifications and language. The inside officers had these procedures down cold, while the rest of us were trying to learn the basics, as well as the elements of the intelligence sector being studied.

In addition to factory markings, country studies, and the in-depth course in map reading, we had a series of written exercises. In each exercise we were given some basic data, then left to analyze it and write our individual reports, such as assessing the nuclear status of India with the information we'd been given. They were all challenging to me, and I took the class very seriously, as if I were earning another graduate degree. This is not to say that I overdid it, but some of the fellows in the class took a less intense approach to the work and to their grades.

I quickly linked up with one of the handful of women in the group, one who was to become a lifetime friend and colleague, both of us pursuing and pioneering the novel path of becoming female operations officers. We were intent on doing well in the course, which for us meant many late nights of study at the Blue U. We began to notice early on that we were among the few who were studying and who were around well after normal business hours. We were learning, among other things, the complex histories of the Chinese and Russian revolutions. One night, in preparation for a test the following day on Mao and the Long March, we stayed particularly late, essentially memorizing the history of the Long March and the early days of Maoism in what became Communist China.

We were alone in the Blue U classroom, and though we speculated that perhaps we were not as bright as our male colleagues and thus had to study longer, we were fairly certain that they were just more risk-oriented, a trait that would prove important in the course later on. Finally, we collapsed and went home, to return the next day to answer an essay question on China on the Long March. We both did well on the test, which pleased us. But so too did our male chum, a class comic, who answered the question about the march with a short essay stating, "The Long March: It was long." He insisted to us that that represented the totality of his response. We then learned that he had received the same grade as we. Hmm. And so, while we soon realized that most of us were going to pass the course with or without nighttime study, the two of us were just too new to this part of the male world to take a chance on winging it.

At this time, I began to have my first experiences with what was later diagnosed as migraine headache. I failed to take proper action because of concerns about my reputation in those early days; I was afraid to tell anyone I had headaches for fear they would think I couldn't deal with stress. So when an attack came on, I would sneak into the projector room, where we were shown training films, and rest in a dark corner on a piece of soft carpet. Heaven forbid I should take leave and go home with a headache. I quickly learned to keep up a façade throughout these painful sessions. I kept this up for a number of years, until I was able to get medical treatment. Even then I did not discuss the headaches at the office, just worked through them so as not to appear weak. Sometime in the late 1980s treatment for migraine began to advance and people, including me, actually admitted having them and learned of their chemical origin. Thereafter, I took leave and whatever else I needed to contend with them. Times had begun to change, at least among some of the younger, more modern set.

CHAPTER FOUR

THE FARM—OPS TRAINING

Before I knew it, we had finished the academic portion of the course and were off to "the Farm," the Agency nickname for our training site. The entire class, including those who would ultimately work for the other CIA components than DO—the Directorate of Intelligence (DI), the Directorate of Science and Technology (DS&T) and the Directorate of Administration (DA)—attended the short orientation in clandestine training as part of the overall CT course.

All I had heard about the Farm at this point was that its identity, purpose, and locale could not be revealed, and that it was such a clandestine site, a place so secret, that it was rumored to have "black houses" stashed around the grounds, lived in by Soviet and other defectors who needed to remain in hiding for security reasons.

When I arrived there in late 1967, I was given a new last name, an alias, which I would use throughout the training, and a military uniform to wear for my time at the Farm. The alias would ensure that my true name and those of my colleagues could not be exposed after training, when we all went off to different parts of the world in varying career directions, and might run into each other in some obscure locale. I wasn't particularly keen to wear an army uniform, but it did solve the problem of what I should wear each day and of carrying a lot of suitcases to the Farm for my stay.

The small cadre of women who went to the Farm with the large class of male colleagues roomed in what was then the Women's Dorm. Having never lived on a coed campus, I found it disconcerting to hear some of my male classmates howling my name somewhere in the fields outside my bedroom at night. I don't know whether I was flattered or not. In the line of career guidance, my father had some years before suggested to me that if I were not married by the age of twenty-eight, I should consider getting a serious job. I was getting dangerously close to that age, but howling did not exactly portend the kind of relationship I had envisioned for myself. Regardless, I managed to sleep, but I made the firm decision that I would not, under any circumstances, date anyone in my training class. I already had a boyfriend in Georgetown, so I wasn't particularly worried, but nonetheless I threw down the gauntlet on that matter.

The orientation course consisted of operational exercises, including how to conduct surveillance, but it did not provide the kind of detail that would be covered in the longer session that was only for those going directly into the Directorate of Operations (DO). Much of the month, and certainly a large portion of my time, was spent learning the myriad forms of clandestine written communication. We had different formats for all kinds of reporting. We used cables for information that was meant to arrive at Headquarters at the fastest speed, dispatches for slower correspondence, as well as reports for analytical pieces, and a variety of memoranda and other formats. Each piece of "traffic," as the correspondence was called, had to include appropriate cryptonyms, or classifications, all known to us as "slugs." As during my Blue U days, I spent endless hours learning these basics and less time on the real operational substance. It was like studying a new language, with so many unusual styles, words, and a special vocabulary for the operations, along with all the required security procedures. This was new to all of us.

In spite of the unique atmosphere of the training—the fact that it was a CIA clandestine training site—I felt that the experience was just a continuation of my education, more learning and more new material. I approached it that way and was happy that I did because there was indeed a real learning curve, and once through it, one could focus on the substance, i.e., the operational work itself.

There were two phases of Farm training for the women who planned to make a career in the DO, and three phases for the men. Those CTs who were not planning on DO careers took only the month-long orientation course. We few women who made up that small percentage of our training class who would go into the DO would then continue into a longer course on clandestine operations, also held at the Farm. Only the men would attend a paramilitary course in addition.

Thus, when we completed the month at the Farm, the DO men stayed on for paramilitary training, or PM, as it was known to us. The non-DO students went back to Washington to their new components and began their real jobs. The DO women returned to Washington for an interim assignment before rejoining the men for the long operational (ops) course that would be held at the Farm following the men's PM training.

As noted, none of us females took the PM course; it was strictly for men in those days. It involved a trek through specific jungles of Panama, as well as jump school and weapons training. It also included extensive work on the so-called Obstacle Course, a set of roadways and acreage at the Farm that, as its name suggests, contained myriad obstacles of all kinds, mostly military in nature. It was the height of the Vietnam War, and a certain portion of our class had been hired for Vietnam. In fact, a number of my classmates were either Vietnam paramilitary "students" or draft evaders who had sought out "other U.S. government" experience in lieu of military service.

Wartime preparations aside, it would have been difficult for the organizers of the PM course to arrange special sleeping arrangements, bathrooms, and the like for the few women involved.

The long ops course, however, was another matter. My female classmates had been accepted into the Career Trainee (CT) program with the understanding that we would be fully trained as operations or case officers, as officers who would recruit and handle agents.

Two of us in particular were only interested in becoming case officers because we were both people oriented and deeply interested in the direct contact part of the work, as well as the imagined excitement of agent recruitment and handling. Now several months into our initial jobs and our training, we were beginning to learn a little more about the DO culture, and coming to realize that there were jobs for men and there were other jobs for women.

We began to hear the general "hallway" chatter that women did not make good case officers. It was said that women could not recruit, much less handle agents, and that we certainly would not be accepted by male agents, particularly in the Third World. The two of us who were intent on becoming case officers could not imagine that this was true. Of course it was easy to think of situations in which a male asset would have trouble dealing with a woman, but surely there must be some who would deal with women and not be threatened or lack confidence in the female handler. In fact, we thought that male-female encounters might be easier to "cover" than clandestine meetings among men.

While our male classmates were at the Farm doing PM, we women were back in Headquarters, where we were hearing rumors that the women would not attend the long ops course. By now, several of us trainees were friends and we were getting upset about this rumor. One of us tracked it down and learned that because of the sudden abundance of Vietnam PM entrants, our class was now "overslotted," and there would not be enough room for everyone to attend the entire ops course.

Who was removed from the class listing? The five females. (The few other women in our original class had already planned to go into the DI.) It was unlikely we would become professional case officers anyway, so the logical place to begin to downsize the class was with us. In the DO, the best women could do was become reports officers and serve abroad in that role—i.e., writing or editing intelligence reports for the male case officers, who held agent meetings to obtain the intelligence.

The Christmas season was coming and I was on my way home to the Midwest for the holidays. As I prepared to leave, I was told that I need not rush back for the long ops course, which would begin in early January. My hopes were dashed, and I had no idea what recourse to take. I had done well in the orientation course and there was no reason for me not to continue in the next phase. Further, that is what I had been hired to do.

While in Columbus, I received a call from Washington telling me to report back immediately after New Year's and to head to the Farm.

We were in the course after all.

It had happened that one of us had previously served abroad with the State Department and had already secured an assignment in the Far East following her training and attendance at the full operations course. When her direct management learned that the course leaders had removed her, they went to bat for her and convinced the CT management to admit her into the class.

She was asked how she would feel being the only female at the Farm for the entire ops course. She was already committed to the upcoming job and thus said she would attend under any circumstances. When Training realized that they would have to put her alone in the women's Bachelor Officer Quarters (BOQ) they reconsidered the entire decision and decided to admit the other four females, along with three others who had previously been lined up for the training. This would fill the women's BOQ and end this temporary problem. I have no idea if there were any other cuts in the class, but it appears that everyone originally scheduled was now in.

In the meantime, as our interim assignments at Headquarters progressed, we heard more and more about the deficiencies of female case officers. In fact, we were having difficulty finding any female case officers with whom we could discuss the realities of this particular career choice. We figured if they did exist, they were probably on overseas assignments. We eventually were able to locate one senior female case officer who was also a senior manager in Headquarters— who, as Chief of Operations, was the number three in East Asia Division—but we could not identify anyone else. Nobody.

Female reports officers, however, could be seen throughout the DO divisions and were able to obtain appropriate overseas slots. In spite of our understanding of why we had been chosen for the

DO and the CT program, we were beginning to sense that the career track for females was different from that for males—reports officers were women; case officers were men. We had not been told this during the hiring process.

CHAPTER FIVE

THE LONG OPS COURSE

We rejoined our male classmates in the new year and started the long ops course. Still in alias and military uniforms, we were also expected to adapt to a new society. By that I mean that we were not just living on a military installation, but we lived a legend, a fake identity. In essence, we continued in our alias identities in the long ops course and lived as patriotic Americans in make-believe countries made up of communist and noncommunist states. They were all individually named and had their geographic boundaries and governments, complete with foreign missions, intelligence services, some nuclear facilities, and specifically named officials. In the legend we would target certain agents from the communist states and try to find ways to get them to spy on their country for the country we represented, which was democratic. It was, of course, a simulation of all the possible scenarios that we could encounter when we went back into the real world on our foreign assignments.

I had no trouble learning the legend or seeing myself as a citizen of the contrived democratic country. In fact I took it seriously enough that I might as well have been assigned abroad in a foreign country. When we were on operational training exercises in this context, we could wear our civilian clothes. When we were not actually doing operational projects in the fake society, we were in military uniform, in classrooms getting lectures on operational procedures and ways of reporting.

I was assigned to a classroom with a group of young men— some of whom were already career professionals, and others, like me, just out of graduate school or some sort of military service, or avoiding military service altogether. One of the more sophisticated members of my "homeroom" had joined the Agency because he expected to spend a career in nation-building, one of the idealistic pursuits of the Vietnam period. He already had some overseas experience and seemed more worldly than the rest of us. He always came to class with a flask, which I had believed to contain coffee. I myself did not need any caffeine to get energized for the day since it was all new and exciting to me. I later learned that his flask held martinis, not coffee. He was a real DO field officer. Over the years, I realized that alcohol was a big part of a lot of DO lives.

We had each been assigned an adviser. Sensing my need for a little moral reinforcement, a couple of male classmates promptly told me that they had heard about my adviser—and that he had a reputation for "hating women". They wished me good luck in overcoming that and left me alone to figure out how to deal with this man. I was definitely on my own!

Some weeks into this portion of the training, I had my first private session with my adviser. We would both be role-playing, with me acting as the case officer and him as an agent from one of the fake communist countries. I was sent to a room in the men's dorm that had been converted into an office and sat down, alone with this man who would oversee the beginning stages of my career development. The walls were covered with *Playboy* centerfolds and various other pictures of sexy, minimally dressed women. I assumed it was one of the guys' rooms and that they just had to have those pictures around. I did notice that my adviser seemed distinctly uncomfortable.

I had also been told that, while hating women, he could also be flirtatious. I was concerned about that since I did not want any problems with my reputation and my relationship with my adviser. I'd already had one warning on my interim and didn't want anyone to think that I was available or "easy." I wasn't verbally direct at the time, but at one point early on in this first game-playing session, I had to assert my authority and show him that I was a take-charge kind of woman, I asked that he not use profane language with me. He had used the phrase "cul-de-sac" to describe a meeting site. At the time this phrase was not in my lexicon, but I had had enough foreign language skills to recognize what had to be a reference to a female reproductive organ. So I asked him to use another word to describe the meeting site. Unfortunately, he immediately saw where I had gone off track and politely explained to me exactly what a cul-de-sac is. By now I was beginning to feel very comfortable with my adviser, who was playing his role as a foreign agent, and to suspect that he was neither a woman-hater nor a womanizer. In fact, he was remarkably nice to me, considering his reputation. Although I kept waiting for the other shoe to drop, he continued politely after this training exercise to outline the purpose of the training and the goals I should achieve. It all sounded exciting and challenging.

All in all, the initial session went well in spite of the wall displays, the cul-de-sac, and my own nervousness and discomfort. My adviser remained polite and supportive throughout the ops course.

Later that evening at the Student Lounge where we CTs met to socialize and review the events of the day, amid the fast-flowing gossip, I heard that two of my classmates had been "called into the Front

Office" to be reprimanded. To my surprise, their crime had been the centerfolds in the office where I met my adviser in our game-playing exercise. Apparently they had made a special effort to decorate their dorm room in such a colorful and suggestive way to ensure a challenging first meeting for me. I had tried to remain calm in the meeting, but my adviser had been extremely offended by the pictures and had reported the incident to management. Needless to say, my adviser turned out to be a fine gentleman, a family man and father of seven, who could not have been more supportive over the ensuing training period.

Strange things continued to happen during the long ops course. One of my male buddies and a confidant in those early days was suddenly dismissed from the course for, among other things, eating his "recognition signal." This is a device used to identify yourself to someone (e.g., an agent) you do not know but need to meet. My chum had devised his operational plan and chosen a pear as his recognition signal. His agent had been provided with a description of him and his signal. Apparently, however, when my friend went to the meeting site, he became nervous and ate his pear while waiting for the agent to surface, thus failing to make the meeting. Sometime later, and presumably after further failed efforts about which I was not informed, he was told that he did not have the qualifications to make a good operations officer and was dismissed.

Another colleague, on a surveillance exercise in a nearby Virginia town, jumped over a hedge into a private yard after his surveille' (which we called a rabbit) had turned around and walked back toward him. In his panic as surveillant not to be identified by the rabbit, he leapt over the hedge, only to find himself facing a moving lawnmower and its owner. He later told us that he just picked himself up, dusted the grass off his clothes, and said "Good morning" to the stunned gardener. There was no negative fallout from the meeting.

I myself had a small misadventure when, while walking down a suburban sidewalk during one training exercise, I stopped and pretended to be feeding a parking meter in an effort to mislead my rabbit. As I inserted a coin, the apparent owner of the car parked in the spot I had chosen appeared and asked me what I was doing. I don't know if my rabbit noticed this brief encounter as he kept moving. Hopefully not, since the idea was that the rabbit should never be aware of the surveillant. Since it was a training exercise, life was not at stake, merely my grade on this particular exercise. Never mind that we conducted it in a real place with normal people. I didn't get a negative critique on my performance, so I figured my rabbit had not seen the encounter.

I've often wondered about some of the strange occurrences that happened in these Virginia suburbs, as well as a few others around the nation, that we used in our training exercises. I never heard of any complaints, but some locals must have wondered why there would occasionally be a sudden surge of activity in their quiet neighborhoods.

For example, when following our surveillance target, the rabbit, we used positioning which allowed a segmented cluster to follow the rabbit at any one time. If the rabbit ever turned on the surveillant and made eye contact, you failed the exercise, the assumption being that the rabbit had identified you. But there were always others in the surveillance team, allowing for one to be spotted and drop out while others carried on the surveillance. So if the rabbit chose to enter a store, perhaps one with little activity, the pursuer would follow him in ███████████████████████████████████ ██████████████████. I remember one such exercise in which the rabbit went into a specialty antiques store that barely appeared to be open. He was followed in a certain sequence by the team, with each person approaching the only person present asking for something in the store. The poor owner must have been impressed at the sudden business surge, but disappointed when there were no purchases and when all his customers quickly disappeared.

At the end of the long ops course, we had a "Final Problem," basically an exam for the entire training. For this exercise, the whole class was divided into groups to carry out a simulated operation from beginning to end. This meant that we would have a fake station, along with targets, agents, and recruitment exercises, for which we would write reports and cables and carry out a range of technical activities, essentially performing the gamut of activity that could be used in a real operation overseas.

And so off we all went to our different locations to set up our mini operations.

One of my classmates, a former Marine with real leadership potential, not among my cadre, was in the last stages of this final ops project. By this time his group had identified, surveilled, phone-tapped and made direct contact with the prospective agent. They had assessed the target's potential in terms of access and reliability, referred to as "vetting." Through a series of meetings, they had also developed a relationship with him under a cover scenario. This phase is referred to developmental work and rapport building. They were now ready to make the recruitment pitch to the target—the big moment in operations. This stage was and is considered the heart of the clandestine business and is the basis on which the quickest promotions are made.

The Marine, who was also rightly chosen to be team leader, set up a meeting with the target in another room. In the adjoining room were his colleagues, who were listening in through the devices they had set up next door. During the meeting, the team leader, now acting as a case officer (CO), identified himself to the target as a CIA operative. He then went into his pitch about the quality of the organization, its importance, and the critical contribution that this potential agent could make if he agreed to work for the CIA—that is, to commit treason against his own country.

To convince the foreigner to whom he was now making the critical recruitment pitch of the professionalism of his organization, he and his colleagues had agreed that someone would knock at the meeting room door at a precise time and deliver a message of specific interest to the target. This would demonstrate the skills of the recruiter and his parent organization, the CIA, and hopefully lead to the last step in recruiting the agent.

The case officer's meeting was proceeding well. When the colleagues in the adjoining room heard the CO and the target at a certain point in their conversation, one of them left the adjoining room and tapped on their meeting room door. The CO went to the door to receive the message and prove himself to the target. In so doing, he stepped outside of the room, only to feel the door slam shut behind him.

He turned around and pounded on the door, asking the target to open up and let him back in. Whether the target responded promptly or not we never knew, but the CO told us all later that he had indeed succeeded in recruiting the agent, even though his professionalism was seriously diminished by his Marx Brothers–like effort to prove his credentials. It was a one-off episode, and it did not prevent this officer from rising to the most senior ranks of the Clandestine Service.

While my own group carried out this project in another set of rooms, I had a problem. Unfortunately, I had the misfortune to get a ferocious migraine right in the midst of the operation. I participated in the initial surveillance exercise and in wiring our rooms so that we could listen to the room next door, where our teammate would recruit the agent. The wiring consisted of taking out the medicine cabinet and putting wires through and behind it to the adjoining room.

I was not team leader and so agreed to stay in and monitor our room a good part of the time. Someone had to be there at all times since we had so much valuable and classified equipment with us. With my bad head, I was chosen to remain behind to ensure that no one entered. At one point, leaving the bathroom. I noticed that one of the plastic clips holding up the medicine cabinet was broken, perhaps by us. I leaned over to try to adjust it, and the whole cabinet, mirror and all, crashed to the floor, making a horrific noise as it hit the tiles.

I soon heard a knock on the room door. It was maintenance who had heard the crash and was inquiring if anything was wrong. Needless to say, I was not supposed to draw attention to our rooms or our activities. I said I had just dropped a heavy suitcase and that everything was fine.

In the meantime my unwitting colleagues were out on the streets surveilling the target. I did confess to them when they returned that I had had a little mishap—they couldn't have missed it anyway, since there was a large empty space now on the bathroom wall, with some wires quietly protruding out of it. We reinstalled the cabinet and everything looked just as it had before. Training exercise aside, it would not have been good to have to explain myself to building management. My group was not mad at me, assuming fairly that they may have misattached the clip when they reinserted it, never mind that I had jiggered with it.

CHAPTER SIX

BROTHERS AS AGENTS

I left my virtual world at the Farm every weekend and usually returned to "normal" life as a young single woman living in Georgetown in the late 1960s. Somehow I kept it all very neatly separated.

Often we would borrow special tradecraft equipment so that we could practice using it over the weekend. On one of those occasions, instead of going back to Georgetown, I made a visit home to my family in Columbus, Ohio. For homework, I signed out and took with me a large and fairly ugly pocketbook—a "concealment device" (CD)—that had a camera hidden in the bottom,

At the time, my youngest brother, Richard, was eleven years old and was the only one of my siblings still living at home. I was happy to see my family and stayed up late chatting with my parents, who knew about my secret employment since I had not been advised not to tell them when I initially applied. They understood that I was in training, but at a locale I could not identify. And they also knew that I could not discuss any aspect of my work then and thereafter. We lived in a large and very secure house, not to mention a safe neighborhood in the suburbs. While usually obsessively conscientious about this equipment, I apparently left my pocketbook on the stairway to my bedroom.

The next morning, I was awakened early by my little brother, with the words, "Where did you get the cool pocketbook with the camera hidden in the bottom?"

I know these were his exact words because I will never forget them. I was horrified that he had discovered my CD. My immediate reaction was denial, but Richard was quite clear that the pocketbook was mine and had a camera hidden in it. He asked if it was "for my secret work at the Pentagon." Now I was even more horrified. My cover job was as a civilian at the Pentagon, but he didn't know that. He had basically guessed my cover and undone my early exercise in tradecraft.

Barely awake, I finally managed to reverse the situation by putting him on the defensive with the question, "What were you doing in my pocketbook?" It worked. He quickly explained that he had been looking for something in Mother's purse and had mistakenly gotten into mine. Now he was uncomfortable too. It was my first experience of a professionally compromising situation. I made it very clear to him that I would not mention this incident if he did not. Mother certainly wouldn't approve of his rifling through her pocketbook! For extra security, I said that I could be killed if he ever told anyone about the purse. I did feel bad about that lie, but not as bad as I felt about having been discovered. I was desperate.

All weekend, Richard and I passed furtive looks at each other, and I wondered if an eleven-year-old in the Midwest could really bring my fledgling career to a halt. Fortunately, he was the most discreet of relatives and never mentioned the matter to me again, until I raised it years later. He explained that he had identified the pocketbook immediately because it was so large and ugly—and he "had seen things like it on *The Man from U.N.C.L.E.*"

I might as well have been in Communist China, given my horrified response to the incident and my efforts to obfuscate.

This very same brother revealed even more skills at tradecraft when, following training at the Farm, I went home for a spell, now engaged, before getting married. I spoke to my then fiancé every day on the phone, in often long and romantic conversations. One night my brother made reference to something I had said that day to my fiancé. I asked him how he knew about that remark. He was forced to admit to me that he had been listening to me on the telephone. In fact he had been listening to every conversation I had with my fiancé. He had learned—perhaps from *The Man from U.N.C.L.E.*—that he could listen to a telephone conversation, and not be heard himself, if he unscrewed the mouthpiece of the phone he was listening on. By this time, my youngest brother was twelve, and I was getting used to his skills.

With three brothers, and no sisters, I was probably well equipped to end up in the career I did. Not only did I have my young phone-tapper, but another brother had used me for BB gun practice during our teen years. He invariably would be in a shooting match with our neighbor, Billy, and somehow they both had access to these guns. I was always cautious when I saw this particular brother hanging around outside when I got home from school. And, indeed, one day I got caught in the crossfire between him and Billy. He hit me in the corner of the eye, but later apologized, saying that he meant to hit me in the torso. Luckily my eye survived. I don't know where Mom was, because she was a very conscientious mother. But since she had grown up in a family of four sisters, she didn't know much about boys.

CHAPTER SEVEN

FIRST ASSIGNMENT— CHINA OPERATIONS

Following the long ops training, we all went back to Headquarters, to the assignments that would actually begin our careers. Though I had done my graduate work on Latin American and spent a summer in Argentina, I had already done a three-month interim on a Central America desk, where I tried to keep track of some of the guerrillas—then known as Marxist-Leninists (ML) in a Central American country. In spite of my studies, I decided early on that I could not see myself pursuing guerrilla movements in Central America. I wasn't really certain they represented as big a threat as my colleagues believed, nor was I convinced that communism would spread into and take over Latin America, regardless of Castro and his missionary, Che Guevara. I simply did not believe the domino theory applied there, which is not to say that I didn't think there were concerns and areas to be energetically pursued. But by now, I also understood the LA Division to be very disinclined to take female case officers.

Despite my background, I began to think that my time would be better spent on more definite and hostile Cold War subjects such as China or the Soviet Union. I opted for China Operations, a major component of the East Asia Division. The chief of China Ops had shown direct and specific interest in hiring me, and I was impressed with his attitude about potential female case officers.

I knew little of substance about China; certainly I had no specific expertise. But it was a critical nation at the time, and I thought I could learn enough to do an effective job. And so I began to familiarize myself with a country that came to fascinate me and about which I could develop some genuine concern. It was a remarkable time— the end of the Cultural Revolution and a period in which China was an absolute Denied Area (an area under unfriendly control) for the United States.

Adding to my decision to go to China Ops, the Division "had a successful senior female officer." I had already heard of this capable woman, who had risen to the upper ranks of China Operations, in fact to the number three position in East Asia Division, as Chief of Operations. She was described to me so often that she took on legendary proportions. While she was not the chief of the entire component, she was in a senior management position, and, more important, she had actually served abroad as an operations officer. She had even been successful, according to legend, in recruiting several valuable Asian assets. With this background, she returned to Washington where she was assigned a senior management job in the East Asia Division. I was particularly impressed with her because she seemed to combine the elements I valued and admired—the professional skills and success, along with an appearance of femininity.

It would be a number of years before I learned of another woman reaching the level this woman achieved when I was at the beginning of my career. She was indeed a role model. I simply never imagined that she was and would remain so rare. I could not understand or believe that a competent woman would not have solid career opportunities. My ignorance on this subject prevented me from seeing that my own career options were severely limited—and that this was virtually unchangeable. My blind spots were very much behind what became my own slow career progression. What was actually happening in the workplace, and, most pointedly, in the DO, was so limiting for women that I failed to believe I was perceiving it accurately. I was sure that performance would enable me—and any other basically competent female—to progress in an upward direction. I was not expecting to run the organization, but I was anticipating growth and opportunity with concomitant reward. I was wrong. But I never gave up.

My first assignment in China Ops was to . I was astounded at the limitations of our access.

I still retained some confidence from my college days and, in short order, wrote a paper questioning our policies and asking why we were not looking at opportunities to meet or speak with select Chinese rather than continue what seemed to me a dangerous level of noncommunication. Somehow the paper got to the Front Office—probably because my immediate management did not want to totally quash the enthusiasm of its young woman and new CT graduate.

The paper came back with a flattering remark from the big chief, who wrote that he liked my views and wanted to discuss my paper with a larger section of the staff. As fate would have it, I had accidentally aligned myself with the thinking of some of the top U. S. policymakers, as I was later advised that the Secretary of State and a handful of key officials were working on broadening contact with China. It was the beginning of "Ping-Pong Diplomacy," and I had stumbled upon it by the accident of my own analysis and concern.

I did not know this, of course, and, regardless, I was in intelligence, not policymaking. That was the turf of the Department of State, not the CIA. So I accepted my first "real" job, where I was assigned to a covert action office in the China section. In the public domain, covert action could be known as advertising or public relations. We did not want Marxism-Leninism—in Chinese, Soviet, or Cuban form—to win the hearts and souls of others in the non-aligned world.

My chief enthusiastically assigned me the job of developing a covert action program ███████████████████████████████████ ████████████████████████████ in a certain Latin American country ███████████████████████████████████████ ███ ██████████████████████████).

While I did not see this as a terrible threat to the U.S. government, I was nonetheless able to work up considerable enthusiasm for my new job. I studied what little information we had.

After my initial excitement over the challenge of this first assignment began to subside, I started to doubt that I could accomplish my mission. I was very goal-oriented and had never failed at academic or other assignments. But it was beginning to look as if I could not come up with a workable plan for my project. I proposed various ideas, but was getting nowhere. In the first place, I had virtually no information to work with, since we had limited exposure and thus extremely limited knowledge of the modus operandi of my targets, diplomatic or otherwise. Secondly, the targets were not allowed to venture out alone, but had to go about in groups of at least two while on foreign assignment. This made things difficult.

I presented as many ideas as I could to my chief, and he kept telling me not to lose my enthusiasm, to keep coming up with new suggestions. Needless to say, I did not succeed. And they did not succeed in an ideological takeover of the government involved. All in all, it was a successful lose-lose situation.

But, at the time, I was disappointed in myself for not accomplishing the desired goal in my first assignment. Everyone concluded that this was all right; it had been a big order. But, by now, I was also married. I was then assigned to a job that required more writing and analytical skills—"a girl's job," as they said in those days.

In short order I found that my desk had been changed. I came in one day to learn that I had been assigned a desk in an open hallway corridor with several other women. My own desk, which had been in a small, private office with a window, had been given to a male colleague of my same age and rank. I was disappointed, but was told that our staff was growing and they needed my desk for a newcomer. In retrospect I realize that I did not say much of anything, since I was too busy being polite and assuming that good work would be rewarded once I got going in my job. In fact, it was the beginning of a cool wind that would blow on me throughout most of my career. There simply was no place for women in ops. Females did analytical work and were good researchers. They could not deal with agent, assets; they could not win the trust of others, etc., ad nauseam.

It still did not occur to me that this was entrenched thinking, as I had no doubt that women were as capable as men in dealing with other people and in developing and running projects or programs. I was aware that one had to be concerned about the male ego and behave in such a way that the man thought he was in charge and that his ego would not be damaged. But I couldn't imagine that I or any other female was all that threatening. We were just a mix of different people, with a range of skills and capabilities. I didn't for a minute think that women had an edge on "research and analysis," and that they were "good at detail work" and "intuitive," as I heard endlessly in the coming years. I certainly didn't consider myself particularly so. Nor did I think I was more skilled at detail and analytical work than my male colleagues. I just didn't get it.

A female physician friend at the time wondered if I had chosen a career where it was impossible to progress. She asked me, "Are you trying to be the first female airline pilot?" I was taken aback by the question, since I viewed her with great respect for her medical degree and developing career in medicine. She suggested that she had taken the "easy" route, since there were already some female doctors, and while there were not yet women's dressing areas in the ER, there were places where the young female doctors could change clothes and sneak in an occasional nap while on twenty-four-hour duty. She had chosen a career where women had already been accepted. I pooh-poohed her question and never gave it any substantive thought, since it had seemed so silly. But I have not forgotten it.

I had a clever and very amusing boss at the time, perfect for covert action because he was so imaginative and creative. He also "liked the girls," as they used to say, and I was among them. As a now newlywed I figured I was pretty uninteresting to men. A ring on the finger did make a difference in how some men viewed me, and in fact several old pals just stopped calling me altogether. I was happy in my marriage then and didn't need the extra attention from extraneous Romeos. However, I soon learned that my boss was interested in me.

He arranged a business trip to New York—TDY (temporary duty) for me and him and a few others on our desk. At first I didn't suspect anything, but when we arrived at our destination and checked into the hotel, I found that his room was next to mine, and the rooms of my fellow travelers were all on another floor. By now I was suspicious—and nervous. This was my boss, and I was happily married, and I didn't care to get involved in any shenanigans anyway. I feebly tried to change the location of my room with some talk about finding a less costly one, but I was really on weak ground as I maneuvered, since he was standing right beside me and was in charge of the TDY, expenses and all.

We went to dinner as a group, and I was feeling a little more comfortable about the situation. I was also plotting ways to get back to the hotel with the other guys and get into my room alone. As dinner ended, the men all went in different directions, except for the boss. I couldn't believe it. They must have agreed to this—or sensed that the chief had his own agenda. Maybe they all really had other plans, but I doubt it.

So, back we went to the hotel, getting into a hot and heavy conversation as we walked. In fact, the discussion was steamy by the time we reached the hotel. I was always loathe to get anyone angry with me, particularly a supervisor. I consistently tried to wiggle my way out of any awkward situation, essentially by pretending it was not awkward and coming up with an appropriate alternative. In this case, by the time we got to our rooms, I was feeling guilty just for talking with this man, who clearly had sex on his mind and was beginning to make me think about it too. I did like him and found him very amusing, but I wasn't planning to do anything about it. I was married! I got back to my room intact after rattling off a series of excuses for ending the evening. I sat there alone for the rest of the night, wondering how I had gotten into this situation and what I had done to get this guy on such a jag. I didn't know whether to be more concerned about my husband or my job future, though I didn't really think this man would harm me professionally. But I did think he might not be as supportive of me as he had been.

The next morning I was feeling so upset by the previous night's conversation and the direction my relationship had taken with my boss that I dreaded even going to our meetings. In fact, whether it looked good or not, I decided I would be a little late to the session just to avoid any direct contact with him. This way he would be involved in directing the meeting when I got there and wouldn't be able to give me the slightest attention.

I was wrong. He was late too. In my carefully scheduled late plan—twelve minutes—I had not considered that he might be late as well.

So when I walked out of my hotel room and went down to the lobby, who should I see but my boss and a prominent man from the movie industry, whom I recognized. My boss looked over at me, and of course I had to join them. He introduced me and said, "He knows about us." I gasped and sputtered back, "There is nothing to know!" I saw the faintest smile on my boss's face as he explained that the movie man knew where we worked. I was not a woman of the world.

CHAPTER EIGHT

MARRIAGE

This won't take long.

On the personal front my life lurched along. As noted, though I'd definitively decided that I would not date anyone in my CT class, once in training at the Farm, I now had more male friends than I'd ever had in my life, given my prior limited experience in coeducation. I was casually dating someone back home in Washington, but by this time I was increasingly distracted from Georgetown by my training and the male colleagues I was getting to know at the Farm.

Suffice to say that I basically fell in love with a classmate who was fun and funny. Yes, fun and funny. That seemed enough to build a lifelong relationship on. As I said, I was not experienced, in spite of the impression my boss on my early interim assignment had of me. The connection with my beau was powerful, and I hadn't initially realized that he was in fact quite married. Nonetheless, and my traditional values aside, we proceeded. Two years later, we got married, though at the time I had a bad case of mononucleosis, misdiagnosed by my doctor as fatal Hodgkin's disease. Well, I did live, but I was wiped out.

Now married and still working the China desk, I realized that I would not be taking an overseas job relating to China, as I would travel and work with my husband, wherever he got assigned. So I decided to make a job change in Headquarters until we got our joint overseas assignment.

In the meantime, my husband started getting job offers from his home base, Africa Division. I wondered what they would offer me.

Nothing.

I was soon advised that they did not do "tandem couples," couples with dual, co-located assignments. It had never occurred to me that we would not get a joint assignment. I eventually suggested I could go out under cover as a "housewife" and teach in a university. Nothing could have been easier than housewife cover—two for one, two at the cost of reassigning one family. All the woman would have to do would be to join women's clubs, local activities, educational institutes—and from there develop contacts that could lead to operational targets for herself, for her husband, or for another colleague. It was so simple and so basic.

Bad idea. Absolutely not. My idea was too avant garde for this generation, though it had seemed to me to be very practical.

To be fair, my husband was getting stressed that he couldn't go overseas, at least not with me. Eventually Headquarters offered him a position in the Washington area ███████████████ ███████████████ working against hostile nations of interest to us. He was away lot, but that was part of the job, and I was okay with it.

As my work situation became more fulfilling, I was beginning to see less and less of my husband. By now we were both busy in our careers, and he was no longer in the Headquarters building, so

I didn't see him during the daytime as often as I had. I was relieved that he had a good operational assignment, because I wanted him to have job fulfillment and excitement in the work he had so looked forward to, especially because I was still on a medical hold and feeling increasingly guilty about keeping him from getting the overseas slot he wanted. But we were married, and the idea was to work together.

I did think it odd when one night he put some of our stereo equipment in his little VW to take to his office the next day. I suggested it wouldn't be safe in that car, parked on the street, especially since we lived in an area of Alexandria, Virginia, that was on the brink of gentrification but not yet there. But I could tell he did not want to hear that from me, referring to my questions as he often did as "insecure" or "jealous," so off went our stereo system. And a few other things, I later realized.

Just before my Valentine's Day birthday, he said, "We need to talk." Where was he taking me for my birthday, someplace lovely, I was guessing. No, he had to tell me that he had "gotten his alias identity mixed up with his true identity" and in that situation had become sexually involved with his agent. To say I was devastated would be an understatement, but my life changed that day, and, largely by my own choice, I never saw him again. Not to mention that he took a P.O. box, so I couldn't have found him anyway.

Stunned, I decided I'd have to live through this one, but I certainly had no idea where to go from here. I went to the office the following Monday and soon enough various people were around, letting me know that they had seen this coming, that they knew he was having an affair with someone else. Apparently I was the only person who didn't know. And I was working in a hotbed of gossip. I don't think gossip is more popular and prevalent anywhere than in the DO, except maybe Hollywood.

Now on my own again, I soon realized that I couldn't even get a credit card in my name. I had no choice but to rearrange our mutual bills so that they would be in my name, and I would begin paying. He had left me $125 to cover expenses since he knew I had not been prepared for this sudden development. To my amazement, when I called the telephone company they said they could not give me a phone in my name until "permission" was obtained from my husband to release his name and put the phone in my name. This was the beginning of my efforts to establish a name for myself as a single woman. I could not believe it.

CHAPTER NINE

COVERT ACTION

In the meantime, while married, I had left the China desk with its international travel potential and decided that I should take an assignment that enabled me to stay "domestic" for a period of time, though in fact by this time, I was receiving no more offers for overseas assignments from anyone. I began a new job in the Covert Action (a clandestine action undertaken to influence the course of political events) Staff. It was a component filled with some of the most colorful and talented employees of the DO and some of the most interesting work.

As fate would have it, my CA career began amid the *Ramparts* exposé. Covert Action had been one of the most colorful and active components of the DO and the Agency in its early days, but in the late 1960s, a news magazine called *Ramparts* wrote about CIA involvement in the international student and labor movements. It exposed CIA support of front groups, including the National Student Association. It was the beginning of a dark period for the CIA's Directorate of Operations and the entire Cover Action activity. Slowly it would unwind, but not yet.

The relationship of the Agency with U.S. media gradually underwent a sea change. It was no longer possible to have a relationship with U.S. media or any person affiliated with media. Contrary to popular opinion, the Agency did not use the American media and in fact took every legal step possible to avoid any involvement with it that could be construed as having been initiated by CIA.

By now, I was in a serious job and was happy in CA as well as politically innocent and not involved in any of the programs under scrutiny. I was running an international media program and a book program. Neighboring colleagues in the staff were overseeing one of the most significant projects of the day. It centered around the Soviet dissident program, which we spoke of loosely as "samizdat." The word and practice of samizdat dates back to tsarist times and has long been used by the disaffected in Russia and the Soviet Union. We took advantage of the disaffected by preparing propaganda directed at them. It was the height of the Cold War and relations between the U.S. and the USSR were at a low. Samizdat became a key program and one that was wholeheartedly supported on the U.S. side because of widely held negative views about the Soviet Union and life in that country.

Beyond samizdat and my media project, there were other international programs, all of them essentially aimed at alerting the reader to the dangers of international communism, whether Soviet, Chinese, or Cuban. And of course, the rest of the message focused on the positive aspects of democracy and the democratic process, including life in the U.S. This was an easy philosophy for me to get behind, since I saw very clearly the negatives of the Soviet and Chinese lifestyles. The repression in China during the Cultural Revolution was particularly oppressive and horrifying. And one had but to remember Stalinist Russia to think of the Soviet system at its worst. I had no philosophical doubts about the programs and their overall direction, even if I understood that democracy as a political system was not necessarily the ideal model for all nations. It was the best that modern man had yet produced, and with its many freedoms, promised a better life for most human beings than did any of the competitive systems around the world. I was a true believer.

Not only was the job gratifying substantively, but it afforded me one of the very few times in my career that being a woman was not a negative. The CA staff had its share of ambitious and competitive officers, but there was no prejudice that I observed or felt against women. I was temporarily freed from the issue of whether a woman could do the job, perhaps because women were already accepted as writers and as creative beings, which enabled this particular component to have a broader, more open-minded orientation. While the leadership positions still went largely to men, women in CA could perform meaningful jobs and even take on some management responsibility.

I met one particular CA asset for lunch once a month, at different locales. He was Latin American, and in spite of constant warnings that "a woman cannot deal with a Latin American male," I had a very successful relationship with this man. At our meetings, we would review his latest article, which covered the hot international issues of the day, but stressed the dangers of communism, especially Castro and Che-oriented communism spreading throughout Latin America, at that time a theme that rang true with many readers and certainly with my own management.

My only problem with my asset was that I had to pay him his monthly fee in cash, and he was very uncomfortable with my doing that in the restaurants where we met, for fear it might appear he was not paying the lunch tab. This would not have been manly.

As we did not meet in a private or covert site, I was forced to give him his cash on a street corner in downtown Washington. Although we changed our location each time, I was always concerned that, if caught, we would have quite a time trying to explain why the young female was giving money to the older gentleman on a Washington, D.C., street corner. I feared that I appeared to be affiliated with the world's oldest profession—not the "second oldest," as we referred to the spy business.

CA was exciting precisely because it was ideological and also because of the immense creativity involved. While I had not been successful in my previous assignment, I was now working in an area where I could actually accomplish something. CA was alive with talent. In the outside world, the public domain, as it is more properly known, some of the people working in CA would have been earning huge salaries on Madison Avenue and wherever major public relations and advertising programs rewarded their employees financially. But that was not life in the CIA. Rather, it was considered a privilege to be able to work for the Agency and to be involved in innovative and influential programs. And it was exciting. Some very well-known Americans, who later went on to other careers, came out of the CA arena, where they'd served briefly. I often read the views of some of these people with interest, knowing that they once worked for the same outfit I now found myself in. But, then, I never thought of leaving. I didn't care about promotions or money in those days, not when I was involved in work that was so satisfying and meaningful.

With the *Ramparts* flap, however, the CA staff was beginning to unravel. Many programs were now exposed and thus compromised. CA had to downsize its personnel and its programs. In many ways, it was the end of one of the most colorful chapters of CIA history. Although CA continued, it was severely diminished from its influential and colorful heights of the pre-1968 era. The *Ramparts* crisis represented a period of break and transition in the history of the Agency. The heyday of our worldwide covert action programs was over. CA was reduced in its intelligence capacity, moved essentially from playing a key role in the Directorate of Operations to being its controversial problem child. Here I was, an ingénue in a play that was about to go way off Broadway.

By this time, I understood that I could not build a long-term career in CA, but I had not yet sorted out my personal life enough to know what direction I should and would be taking. My marriage was over, and I was in a downsizing CA with no other immediate career goals or plans in place.

CHAPTER TEN

AN AREA DIVISION

As usual, I had little control over my own destiny and few ideas how to get it. Like a lot of young women of my era, I respected authority and assumed that my male managers were guiding me in the right direction. My CA chief was a decent man and called me in one day to discuss the downsizing in CA and to tell me that I was not well positioned for career growth since I was not in an "overseas" component. I knew he was right, but at this point, had absolutely no goals for myself, being temporarily lost in the confusion and personal anguish of a not-anticipated divorce.

The chief said he had located another job for me and that it would position me to get overseas within a few years. "A few years." What did that mean?

In spite of some potential in Asia and particularly China Operations, I now understood that it was virtually impossible to be assigned as a female operations officer to Latin America, Africa, or the Middle East. I cannot say how many times I was told that "a woman simply cannot do the job in . . ." Fill in the blank with any geographic area, possibly excluding Europe. And so I went to Europe

Division for the interview. I had adequate French and Spanish to build on.

I had the interview, hoping of course to be positioned as a case officer working on a desk at Langley until the foreign field opportunity appeared. In my interview, I went over my training background and my work in China and CA. But I stressed that I loved languages and would look forward to more training in French, Spanish, whatever they wanted for me.

The interviewer, a manager in the division, seemed interested but in short order said to me, "We already have a woman we like." What?

I think this was one of the most stunning moments of my entire career. I was divorced, could not work in CA, had had no overseas experience, and now was told that I would not be going overseas to Europe, because they already had a woman they liked!

Still, I went to the Europe Division. I had to. I was assigned to a "staff." I did not have the perspicacity at the time to realize that assignment to a staff, essentially a research unit, was a virtual kiss of death for anyone on the move. Over the years, though, I did observe that staff and administrative assignments were areas where women might excel. But I wanted to be in an "action" job, not sitting on a research staff doing what I was beginning to see was widely accepted as "girls' work."

I joined a staff that was handling the care and feeding of the remaining programs and assets in the European piece of certain international labor activities. It was clear to me almost immediately that I would not be handling any agents, but that I would be doing the research and analysis of some of the projects, overseeing the paperwork and the details for more senior men who would travel abroad in TDY status to meet their agents and do what I considered the fun and interesting part of the job.

I shared a room with a gentle lady who came out of the very old school. A woman should be seen but not heard. She was the quintessential little old lady in tennis shoes. She had worked for the Agency her entire adult life and was now ensconced in the depths of the labor program, carrying perhaps the best historical knowledge of anyone in the organization on the players and the programs. She was a prototype—the conscientious, unmarried female who knew all the details of select programs and who stayed put in the job year after year because "she was too valuable" to be let go for assignment to another desk.

Was this who I was on the road to becoming? Because this was not in my game plan, diminished as it now was.

While I do not mean to make pejorative comments about any individual, I could not help seeing what was right in front of me, and beginning to fear the future. I did not want to end up like this woman. Regardless of whether she was fulfilled or happy, she was not living the life I envisioned for myself, even in my most negative moments. I did not want to be an "old maid career woman." But I was beginning to encounter more and more women of this type. They would never advance beyond a certain grade level— generally, a GS-13. And the good ones would then be kept in position because they were "so valuable"—and rewarded with the praise of an often charismatic male chief and with "step increases" instead of actual promotions. (Step increases were small financial increases—ten per promotion cycle—on the way to a promotion from grade to grade within the system. They allowed management to keep these valuable employees while not using up the promotion slots so dearly needed to encourage the more valued, successful male operations officers.)

Meanwhile I was no better suited to work on international labor than on the Chinese People's Liberation Army, but at least I could learn this business, and with study and application, obtain enough knowledge to do a good job. It was just a question of on-the-job training. My manager called me in for my interim review some weeks later and commented on an area where I could improve my work, though I can no longer remember what that was. He happened to give me my review on the very day that my divorce was finalized. I burst into tears. It was one of the few times in my career when I cried. The poor man could not have been nicer, but I was simply unable to hold back. At least I didn't miss any work. It probably would have been a good day—or week—to take some leave, but I never entertained the thought. I was certain that I could not let my personal life interfere with my career. Never mind the fact that it did and had. I can't recall, but imagine the poor man let me go back to my desk and regretted he had chosen that day to give me my review.

Looking back, it is with no surprise that I recall a lack of satisfaction with this job. It was going nowhere and I was going nowhere. Within a few months, I realized that I too would sit on this desk for years to come and not have any chance of an overseas assignment. I was right to be in an overseas division, but I was in a dead-end job.

Gloria Steinem was at her peak, as was Betty Friedan's *The Feminine Mystique*, but Friedan's harshness was threatening. I didn't want to be the kind of woman she was describing. It was the early stages of the feminist movement, and there were only a few voices around. There were no role models for young career women, which I clearly was at this time. Obstruction was everywhere. But so was denial.

There was by now one peer-level DO female case officer in my age group who was achieving the unachievable. She was a fascinating character, distinctly unfeminine (no, that is not an insult), but one who had early in her career managed to get an overseas African posting, which turned out to be extremely dangerous. In fact, when Americans were pulled out of the country, she was the "stay behind," as they say in our business. A junior officer, she was the only one who could remain in the position for certain operational reasons. She was probably not as readily identifiable as CIA as some of her colleagues and would have been less noticeable if she continued in an admin or secretarial job as cover, which would appear to have no intelligence connection.

In fact, the situation was so dangerous in the country and she demonstrated a record of good decision-making and courage that she rightly continued in a solid career projection, achieving the first deputy chief slot since the senior woman I had been introduced to earlier in China Operations. But the Africa officer really was a woman of the DO in that she did "men's work" and so demonstrated. She was known for her bowl haircut, for carrying a green book bag, and for her interest in shooting wild game while on foreign assignment. She was the only one of us who was really "cut out" for the DO that we all joined. But she was not a role model for other women, particularly the younger set who were now coming along, with the view that they could have a career, date and marry, perhaps even have children. There were virtually no women like that in the DO career ranks by the late 1970s that I can remember.

As before, I still could not envision that one could not get ahead if one worked hard and effectively. It was not a question of genius, but rather one of basic competence. I still didn't get it.

By now, what little male interest there was in me from my seniors was sexual, not professional. I had lost the support of that early career training (CT) and assignment phase and was beginning to become a "career woman," and a divorced one at that. Not only had I not been prepared for the realities of the professional world, I had been totally unprepared for the morality. I could never have imagined the encounters I would have with my professional male colleagues as a divorced woman. And it is better that I could not. I was now in the ranks, and a divorced, "available" woman in my thirties. None of this was to my liking. But as usual, I did not fully understand the position I was in. I did share some of this with my parents, and my mother suggested people in Washington seemed to be "oversexed."

Though I was still hoping I could get overseas, to somewhere in Europe, the prospects remained dim. There were no offers. I continued in my labor staff job, and my analytical skills grew. That was all that was growing.

I was beginning to see myself in tennis shoes.

CHAPTER ELEVEN

JOB CHANGE—DOMESTIC SERVICE

It was not my first interest, but I had heard about another component, a domestic unit, an anomalous Agency component that collected intelligence from certain U.S. citizens who had a combination of extraordinary foreign access and substantive expertise. Basically this meant contacting American citizens about information obtained, confidentially, relating to national security issues.

Importantly, it was said that women got "real" jobs in this component, and that they even experienced career advancement. While I still had the dream of living and working abroad, I was becoming more pragmatic as I stagnated in my job in EUR.

As to the substance, as the U.S. and the USSR warmed to each other—off and on—during the 1970s and '80s, scientists and other specialists met and learned from each other in the name of science. They often did not like to be encumbered by the limitations and parameters of national boundaries. This is not to suggest any questionable patriotism on anyone's part, but merely to say that those of us in government do not see the world in the same way as a scientist dedicated to and expert in his field. Experts speak to experts, I found, and a lot can be learned from those interactions that cannot be obtained from strictly clandestine assets.

In short order, I got an interview with management, and was welcomed to the division, along with four male colleagues from the DO—we were the first "experimental" entrants from the Directorate of Operations category. Numerous officers had had the same initial CT training as I did, but they had not had operational training or experience since they had initially chosen to go to the DI where this office was originally housed, not the DO. There was a definite cultural issue at stake here, but again, I was on a learning curve.

I was no longer working in Langley, which was just as well since I did not want to run into my ex and by now had no idea where he was working. In my new job, I soon saw that there was a cultural difference between domestic service and the clandestine area divisions. The components had different personalities, different characters. My new division was more conservative, but what I noticed most was the absence of exciting "hallway" conversations. I learned a lot from those interactions in the Clandestine Service and missed them. My attitude and approach to work was not initially in line with what I was to see in domestic service. The work ethic was different. In the CS, one was virtually married to the business. There was an attitude of service first, family and personal life second; it was almost a given that you were privileged to work in the CS and therefore did not punch a time clock, were available any time, and would do what the service asked or required regardless of personal circumstances.

By the time I connected with this new division, I had become aligned with the work-comes-first attitude of the CS. I had never gone home at five o'clock and almost thought it odd to do so.

Further, the tools of the trade were different, though the product was equally valuable. In effect, the domestic program involved discreetly contacting U.S. citizens with access to information or persons of national security interest ██████████████████████

██

██

██

██

██████████████████████████

████████████████████████████████████

██

As with the Clandestine Service, the mission of my new office was to gain knowledge of what was going on in countries around the world—politically, economically, scientifically, and technologically—at the time of the Cold War. It was clear that scientists talked with scientists, breaching the issue of national boundaries, and as well that experts could understand and engage with experts in a way that a political scientist could not. While even American scientists and businessmen were restricted in hostile areas—the USSR, China, North Korea, e.g.—during the Cold War, they were the few Americans who had any access to key foreigners.

We never established a professional relationship with a U.S. citizen without advising him/her of our CIA identity and interest. I cannot say how many high-level American businessmen and scientists I contacted over the years and how many times I was able to gain an initial interview. I had few turndowns in the outside world in spite of being female. I had finally found my niche.

███████████████████████████████████████Each person contacted was told that the meeting was confidential and should be treated as such. In turn, we always made a commitment to the contact ████████████████████████████████████

██

██████████████████████████████Future meetings were set up as time allowed for the businessman/scientist and based on the priority of the information to be obtained. In my years in this field, the people I met with always gave me the time and information I needed. A little-known fact, but I quickly learned that we Americans have many patriots.

This all fulfilled the critical intelligence requirement of protecting sources and methods. I took this part of the commitment very seriously from the beginning, and I rarely saw it broken over all the years I worked in the domestic part of the business. Our promise to protect the CIA relationship with the American source or contact was scrupulous.

But it would not be long before Agency life became more complicated.

In the early days, when I first arrived in the new office, the Agency did not advise the U.S. Congress about these relationships or the intel, the substantive information they provided. But during this time, the CIA was coming under increasing external scrutiny. In late 1974, *New York Times* investigative journalist Seymour Hersh reported on a previously classified CIA operation involving Chile. He described what appeared to be illegal "spying" on Americans by their own government.

Following this latest brouhaha, Democratic Senator Frank Church of Idaho created a Senate committee to investigate allegations of elements of the U.S. government spying on its own citizens, ultimately revealing early CIA connections with journalists and civic groups. Church called the CIA a "rogue elephant". The exposé became the first of its kind against the CIA and led to the beginning of major changes within the Agency. The Foreign Intelligence Surveillance Act (FISA) was passed in 1978, and select intelligence committees were created in both the Senate and the House. Executive Order 12036 and later 12333 strictly limited the activities of the CIA and others in the intelligence community in areas relating to assassination attempts and contact with U.S. media, the Peace Corps, and other foundations.

Our rules of engagement became increasingly restrictive, and perhaps appropriately so, with the changing political environment in the U.S. We did not approach American media or journalists. For a journalist to have contact with us, he or she would have to find us and "volunteer" to be met. I have been asked about this so often over my career and realize that most people didn't believe my response, which was as stated above. We did not recruit U.S. media or journalists.

The same was true for the nonsecular world. We did not approach (professionally), recruit, run, or debrief anyone in the religious professions. A religious figure with access to unique information of foreign intelligence value would have to locate one of us and volunteer to be debriefed, as with journalists. This, too, was something that I found few believed when I spoke of it, but it was true.

And we certainly did not participate in any schemes to assassinate heads of state or any key political figures. I do not know everything that went on before my time in the Agency, but I certainly know that assassination was viewed by all of us as "against the law." It was illegal, and we did not engage in any work pointed in that direction at least not in those days. Again, I cannot say how many times I was asked by well-meaning, and often politically liberal, friends why some of the nastiest world leaders remained in place. The question was usually phrased in a way as to suggest that "If the CIA were really an effective organization, so-and-so would not have survived." Well, this simply is not true. The fact that Muammar Gaddafi remained in power in spite of well-known murderous acts had nothing to do with competence but relates directly to the law. Assassination is illegal, and the U.S. government—and specifically the CIA—did not engage in it at that time. To a person, those who asked me this question never believed my response. When someone would ask why Saddam Hussein, for example, survived if the Agency was so skilled, I would always answer as above, and I would usually see the look of disbelief on the face of my questioner.

The management of my new division was relatively enlightened, at least to the extent that they were gentlemen, rather chivalrous, and willing to give me an opportunity to do a good job; there were two senior women in the division as well. Once I got into the ranks, however, I began to encounter the "real men" of my new component. It took me awhile, as usual, to figure out that this was not going to be a neat and straight road ahead.

I immediately started working for a nice, seemingly competent and responsible man barely older than I was. We covered nuclear scientific issues for reporting coming in from our field installations. This meant that we edited and coordinated the production of this particular element of field reporting to ensure that the final report of what was called "raw intelligence" got to the Agency analytical component covering nuclear developments in the USSR and other countries.

But my supervisor, in spite of having a beautiful wife of his own, was hopelessly infatuated with our sexy young secretary. She was quite good at her work and quite married. Unfortunately, my besotted colleague was so taken with her that he spent a good bit of our workday talking about her, almost drooling, while at the same time overseeing and correcting my work, which he was keen on doing. I had really not worked or even studied a lot with men, so I was amazed at the amount of time and focus my supervisor gave to his obsession. Again, I didn't get it.

Who was I and where did I fit in? Well, I was still convinced that basic, good work would pave the road ahead. That seemed crystal clear to me. Divorced and a female, perhaps I would just have to create another case officer model of some sort.

Since I was recently divorced and didn't particularly want to go home at night, I often stayed late at the office—not very late, mind you, but until perhaps six thirty. The one-step-up senior supervisor to the drooler would stop by my desk at five fifteen to say that he was not impressed with my working late. I was abashed, but finally admitted to him that I was newly divorced, not eager to go home, and would be glad to work a little late and finish some of my outstanding projects. He seemed to accept that, but never really took to me, retaining the view that I was just trying to promote myself and was a typical DO case officer not quite in the mold of the new office.

Now resettled, I once again began to focus on getting a field assignment. Like the overseas components, there were the "Headquarters jobs" and the "field jobs". Everyone tried to get "out" to the field. That's where the fun was--where the action was. Generally speaking, in the DO, one viewed time in Washington Headquarters as unpromotable service, but service that was necessary to win a field assignment. It was more or less considered "doing time" until you could get a "real" assignment.

I had pretty much decided that for personal and professional reasons I wanted to go to New York. I also knew that New York was an unpopular career choice for most of my colleagues because of the cost and the family-unfriendly nature of the city. No one wanted to go there. The more I considered the prospect, the more committed I became to getting myself there. I still hoped to meet a good man and get married again. But it was just a vague plan on my part. I really didn't see any aspect of the future clearly, and my goals were getting more abstruse—I wanted professional success and still wanted to have a family. I was sure that I could do it all—have a career and be married and have children. Now I would be satisfied with two kids, no longer four, as I had originally planned. I got that it would be a challenge to have both a career and a family of my own, but it was now the trend of my generation. We had to do it all—the Superwoman era had started, and I was having trouble with both requirements though I was still confident I could manage both.

Regarding a field assignment, understandably and properly, no officer is meant to work in a division just to gain assignment to a specific city or locale. So, in applying for what one really wants, it is necessary to do a little research, first to determine if there is a "slot" or an opening, and second, to see if you will be taken by the field chief in the specific locale. I thought I was on fairly solid ground with my private selection of New York because New York was such an unpopular choice amid my peers. I could play my cards close to the chest and not appear to be limiting my choices of field assignment, since they would clearly be delighted, if not relieved, to find a person who wanted to fill one of the empty New York slots.

As usual, I did not entirely "get it." At the time, I didn't realize that a good part of the equation consisted of winning the support of the resident field chief. It wasn't illogical, but then, weren't we all part of a presumed fair process that would decide the field assignments from Headquarters? Field chiefs were not supposed to have their own little fiefdoms of personally chosen employees. We were, after all, the government, and fairness was part of the process. No one owned their offices; they were just the temporary curators of those sites. Wrong.

Further, I did not understand the game well enough to sense that one should never list one's top choice in first place, unless you knew you had already been chosen for the assignment. In short, if you wanted a specific assignment, you should probably make it number two on your list of preferences. That was the game.

The good news about New York was that there was some history of female officers in that office. One, long since retired, had been rumored to have done an adequate job there. Another, who remained employed, had also done well, though the chief had not much liked her due to her excessive weight. She was given the field assignment, but once there, was left to identify "women's organizations," and other "female" business locales where a woman might identify potential U.S. citizen contacts. Though I had gotten used to hearing that female case officers did not do well in the Third World, or even in Europe, this was the first I had heard that women had a challenge working in the United States.

The New York job began to look increasingly less available to me. While management was, at the time, begging male officers to go to New York, it really did not seem too interested in getting its few female officers to New York, or on any other field assignment, as far as I could see.

To add to my bad luck, I had an interview of sorts with a hot-shot male officer from the New York office. He let me know that my chances of getting to New York were rather slim, in spite of the openings. I asked why. He responded that "they understood" that I liked to shop and they were concerned about the amount of time I would spend shopping instead of working. I was taken aback, and I cannot now recall what I must have said. Suffice it to say that at the time shopping was not one of my hobbies. Since this officer was one of the key players in New York—the "top producer"—I had to take what he said seriously. But he added that he also did not think I could do the job. Again, I asked why. He responded that women could not successfully meet with high-level businessmen, stressing that I would not be taken seriously. Once again, my jaw must have dropped. I was not encouraged when he ended the conversation with this: "You can't do this job, at least I don't want to think you can."

CHAPTER TWELVE

SAN FRANCISCO

That's how I ended up in San Francisco. It may sound like a windfall since San Francisco was everybody's favorite city, stunning and exciting, and I was lucky to get the offer to serve there. But privately, I did not want to move there. I still wanted to go to New York, just as I had secretly desired to get assigned to Paris when I was in the overseas world. Now, I had to accept or put my career on hold. This was the first time that I had actually been offered a field assignment since one to study Chinese in Taiwan just pre-marriage in China Ops. I of course said yes and moved New York and my professional scheming to the back burner. My personal life was definitely not going as planned either, though I still knew I wanted to remarry and have a family.

With this vague and ill-defined sense of my own direction and future, I uprooted myself and moved West. I knew that it was a great city, but I didn't think I would fit in with the hot-tub, flower-child crowd. It was the mid-seventies, and I was not a West Coast person.

When I arrived at the field office, I found out that I was the only female officer. The chief was an intelligent, experienced man with a naval background, and we got off to a good start. He made it clear to me that taking me was "something of a risk," but he also promptly gave me a good caseload and the full opportunity to pursue it.

Within the first year, I became the "top producer" in the office. "Numbers" was the name of the game in this part of the business in those days, and I was a competent writer, had a lot of meetings, and collected considerable useful information, or intel. I was running neck-and-neck with the boys, in fact, ahead of them in production.

When promotion time came around, I got praise for my production but was told that it was too soon for me to get a promotion. I was perturbed when my two immediate colleagues, of the same grade and approximate age, got promoted to the next level. I was top producer and I had done everything I had been asked and guided to do. And I still could not get the promotion.

A colleague warned me that the chief had suspected I might be discontented if I did not get my promotion at the same time as my two colleagues, and he later told me that he had advised Headquarters it would not be good to promote two of the three of us, leaving me out, particularly with my performance record. So I was beginning to see that performance was not necessarily the road to success, at least not for me.

At no time did I revel in the thought that my performance was exceptional or beyond that of anyone who had passed through before me, but I did think I was good and I knew that I worked hard and outperformed some of my colleagues.

The boss did complain to me occasionally about the neatness, or lack thereof, of my writing and the papers that I would forward to him for final editing. He once came back to my office and asked me why I persisted in using staples on my reports, when he had asked before that I use paper clips. I will admit that I was not the neatest writer—I mean my penmanship—and that I had probably missed his initial point about the staples. I had failed to recognize that this was an important issue, my mistake perhaps, but I honestly couldn't imagine that it mattered. Regardless, I "cleaned up" my act and started using paper clips and long-lined yellow legal paper so that he could clearly read my writing.

I reported directly to the deputy chief of the office, a fine gentleman with a lovely family who, like me, had spent years in Ohio. This seemed good to me. He would probably like me and support my work.

By this time, I had a solid workload and was getting quite familiar with international energy and OPEC oil pricing, among other issues. While we did not form policy, I found myself looking at some of the pricing issues and thinking of ways we could gain a better idea of what was going on internationally in the oil markets.

I took the time to write a paper on this and actually was rather proud of the result. It read well and was somewhat innovative in its approach and recommendations. Management encouraged initiative, and I thought I was on the right track with my ideas.

I politely, and somewhat proudly, took the paper to my deputy chief, advising him that I had done a complete review of our access and reporting on international energy issues and that I had come up with some ideas for expanding the quality and quantity of our reporting on this then important topic.

He looked down at my feet. I was wearing slightly open-toed shoes. And he said, "Your feet really turn me on." The only thing I wanted to turn him on was my paper. He put the paper aside and looked up at me from his desk and leered. I had heard tales about him before, but I had not, until now, seen the leer. Perhaps I smiled, I don't know, but I know I cringed inside even if I hid it, which I hoped I had.

And my paper. All that effort—and my positive thoughts about the new ideas. We didn't even discuss them. He never got back to me on the substance of my proposals, even with a refutation or criticism.

When I finally did get promoted a year later, he came up to me at my desk, leaned over, whispered into my ear in a sultry voice, and told me that I had gotten my promotion. The leer was the same, and I was getting accustomed to it. The gentle whisper in my ear overshadowed my delight at receiving the promotion. I was so busy disconnecting from him that it would not have mattered if they had told I would henceforth be running the office.

I honestly did not know if the man was just practicing his flirtations on me, but I was beginning to get queasy at the thought of one-on-one sessions with him. One day when I was studying a map in our main foyer, he came up behind me and ran his fingers up and down my rib cage. I know it could have been worse, but the man made me cringe, and I did not want him near my rib cage.

After one more incident, I finally went to the chief himself to advise that I was having a "little problem" with my immediate supervisor, the deputy. The chief seemed to understand, and said he would work on getting me a better management contact, but he would do it in a way that would not cause the deputy or me any problem. I liked that idea, as I didn't want anyone to know I was having these little problems. By this time, I really liked the content of my work. As I had anticipated, I loved being in the field and I was beginning to get good feedback from Washington on my reporting and was seeing the value of my work.

I began to report directly to the chief. I continued with the same accounts and stopped using staples in my papers. All was going well. But then the chief decided to make me the EEO officer for the entire office. He specifically asked me to work with the secretaries and clerks. I wholeheartedly agreed that these women did not have the support, opportunities, or rewards they deserved. Unfortunately the secretaries resented me and would only feel that more so if I became their EEO officer. It didn't take long for me to understand that they would not particularly appreciate me because I appeared to have it easy. And, in truth, I did have opportunity that they did not have. Plain and simple. I would have done anything possible to help them get advances and benefits, but they would not have known that.

It was still an era in which women were kept divided—and female internecine conflict supported, even encouraged. In those days, women often got some of their rewards out of working for a man. Further, there was a commonly held view—and one that was often true—that you could always get women to talk about each other. It was a kind of divide and conquer approach that actually worked because women themselves were so conflicted about their changing roles and the feminist movement. Most pointedly, there was concern, doubt, fear, envy—a range of reactions toward those few women who were perceived as actually breaking the mold and getting real opportunities. Though I did not exactly feel so myself, I was aware that my situation was better than theirs. And understandably, they did not particularly want to hear my pep talks about the brightness of the future and the new opportunities. There wasn't much hope for them, and there were few, if any, significant opportunities. They knew it, and I got it. But his appointment did suffice to draw a deeper line between the clerical staff and me, a group of people whom I genuinely liked but suspect did not feel the same about me.

In another inspired moment, this chief added to my portfolio the rather strange assignment, announced in our weekly staff meeting, of having me talk to the men about their "language." By that he meant the swearing that went on, particularly among our military inserts. I had gotten pretty used to it and was beginning to find that some of their swearing made me feel better too. We left that meeting, and the military fellows beckoned to me, winked, and asked me exactly how I planned to get them to change their language. I didn't have any particular response, and I think—and hope—we laughed, and that was the end of it. The guys kind of suspected that the chief was trying to divide and conquer us as well, but by this time they were my buddies and kept me informed on what was happening in the office. Their translations of the chief's and deputy's behavior was pretty valuable to me. They got a lot that I didn't. I was definitely odd "man" out, but I had my chums now and I was getting good on-the-sidelines advice.

Even so, the special X-rated language of my closest military chum was so intricate that I usually did not understand what he was saying anyway. Except for the odd explicit swear word, he had his own military language. Another thing I learned about male and female behaviors in the workplace is that women really do not talk differently among themselves than among men—though the substance will be different. Men, I learned to my surprise, and in spite of having brothers, have a separate language from the one they use socially with women. I was kind of enjoying observing this process. I knew the chief would not really grade me on my ability to get the guys to change, but they would let the chief think they had changed just for my benefit. And I appreciated that.

During this time, it seems that my chief had decided his wife was—let me be careful here—not interested in sex. Or so he told me when we were working late at the office one day. He asked me to "go away with him." I wasn't sure where he planned for us to go, but never mind that, I said no. I did try to say it in a gentle way, suggesting that he was wonderful but that I did not think it a good idea to get involved romantically with the office chief. Perhaps I even smiled. I definitely did not get mad at him, swear, or call him a disgusting animal. No, I didn't speak that way. In those days, most women didn't speak harshly to men or tell them to get lost or whatever. You just tried to make sure that, whatever happened, the man's ego was not damaged and you retained good relations. Especially if he was your boss.

Within a few months, my request for another year in San Francisco—I was still early in my tour—came up. I wrote a memo stating that work was going well and that I wanted to take a third year and continue to develop my program. Tours were usually three to five years in those days, rarely two. In fact, if you went home after two years, there would be considerable question about why you had returned from tour "early."

My chief sent the memo back to me with his comments attached—a necessity since he was the supervisor and needed to comment on and approve any memo back to Headquarters.

To my surprise, he recommended that I return to Washington, where he was certain I could make a "solid contribution." I was shocked, since I was still a productive officer and had also established a range of contacts. In a follow-up discussion, he said he appreciated that I wanted a third year, but felt I would do better in Washington and find other opportunities there. ███████████

███

███████████████████████████████████ He suggested that I take a less active role in an operational area that I had also been pursuing, i.e., looking for foreign assets, one for which I was getting praised by components in Headquarters, who were recipients of my work.

In the meantime, one of the big chiefs from Washington came out to San Francisco to review the work of our office and get updated on any personnel issues. He was a gentlemen and had been one of the managers who had been responsible for my joining the division. So I was kindly disposed toward him and trusted him as well. He was genteel and somewhat old-fashioned, offering to escort me out of the office when I left later that day.

During our pursuant conversation, he asked me how I was doing and how my work was going. He praised what he had seen and said he was impressed and pleased that I had joined the division and taken a field assignment. I was one of two or three women in the domestic field by now, and this really increased their numbers on the EEO front.

Eventually I told him that I was having a problem with some of the advances of my managers. I awkwardly reported that my chief had told me about his problems with his wife and was looking for me to help him out. The shocked Washington chief said he could not believe what I was telling him, and that there must have been some sort of misunderstanding. I said I agreed about the wife, but noted that the romantic gestures toward me had been quite explicit and embarrassing, and that I thought my reaction had led the chief to develop a somewhat negative view toward me, one that perhaps influenced his decision regarding whether I would be extended in San Francisco. The big boss and I ended the discussion without further ado, and it was pretty clear that I would continue to work in this particular office with matters unaltered.

Somehow, and at no small cost, I remained for an additional two years. By this time I did not staple any draft reports, and my male colleagues mentored me on how to avoid both chiefs while doing an effective job.

CHAPTER THIRTEEN

AN OP AT LAST

In San Francisco, one of the professional relationships I established was with a successful businessman. I was once again trying to get into operational activity, and this time the chief did not hold me back, though his enthusiasm remained muted. Arrangements were made for me to travel to New York with my businessman contact to broker an introduction to a foreign individual of interest to a New York-based officer. I was excited since this was what I was trained for and I had failed so far to get.

My contact and I arrived at LaGuardia. Fortunately, as I will soon explain, he was picked up in a limousine by a driver. I headed into Manhattan to the hotel the office had arranged for me. Suffice to say, it was not four star. The light bulbs in the bedroom and small bathroom both hung from a skinny wire out of the ceiling; there was no television; and the room was shabby but clean. I don't know what I'd expected, but this was a far cry from the way James Bond traveled. The good news was that my asset was staying in a mansion outside the city with the target.

I passed the evening in my room and was about to go to sleep when the phone rang. It was my contact, stating that he needed to see me right away and would be coming back into the city.

It was after eleven thirty at night and New York was not then a city for me to be wandering around at midnight. Of course I jumped up and got dressed and headed to the place he wanted to meet me, a strip club that he in fact owned. It was uncomfortable, but I was all business and so was my contact as he explained to me that the individual of interest would not be meeting with us the following morning.

"Not meeting with us?" I said, horrified, now realizing that my mission was in fail mode. I took my contact back to the hotel, which he thought was a dump. I had already gotten a room for him and hadn't cancelled it. I gave him his key and told him that our meeting the next morning was still on, no matter what the target decided. He turned to me and said, "I will not stay in this hotel unless you stay in my room, unless you sleep with me."

Did my jaw drop? It must have. I can't remember, but I bluntly refused and went back to my own room, by now nervous over virtually everything that was happening. To thwart a colleague's romantic gestures was one thing, but to thwart those of my contact was another. I was responsible for keeping him happy and successfully developing our relationship so that he would broker an introduction.

My mission was failing.

The next morning, I got up and headed down to the lobby area at eight thirty, where I was to meet my New York–based colleague, whom I of course I did not know. We had agreed by classified communication that we would each be wearing specific and easily identifiable clothing and carrying a certain magazine or newspaper. He reported he would wear a trench coat and carry a copy of *The New York Times*.

Unfortunately, he was not the only man wearing a trench coat and carrying *The New York Times* that morning. So when I went to the hotel lobby a few minutes before our meeting time, I saw several men who met his description. As noted before, I was on the government, not the James Bond payroll. I don't know who frequented this hotel, other than the occasional bureaucrat, but I could guess.

So it was no surprise that I met more than one man in my effort to find my colleague. As I sought him out, I glanced at several identically dressed men, and of course I smiled since I was trying to signal my colleague. Two different men came over to me separately, and, from their initial comments, it was clear that they were not my colleague. I was being mistaken as a member of the"oldest" profession, not the "second" oldest.

Finally, I spotted and spoke to the right man, and we headed into the hotel restaurant to talk and then wait for my contact to appear at nine o'clock.

But he did not show up. I didn't explain the details of the night before to my colleague, but soon said I would go up to my contact's room and see if he was okay; perhaps he had overslept. I got to his door and knocked, frantic that no one was there. Then I heard rustling in the room and was greatly relieved. It was taking him time to get to the door in the small room, but he finally opened it, stark naked.

Was I shocked? Yes, but I wasn't about to show him. I virtually ordered him to get dressed and come down to the restaurant. I don't know where that voice came from but it popped right out of me. And he did indeed get dressed and come down with me to meet my colleague.

By this time, I was beginning to doubt that my TDY would be successful, and I saw myself failing in this small mission and deserving no career recognition. But my contact now behaved, and from then on, things went well. I turned him over to my New York colleague, and they had a successful meeting after all.

I now headed over to the New York office to meet the Chief of Station, a man affectionately known by colleagues as "the Pear," no doubt because of his general body shape.

I had an additional ulterior motive in wanting to meet with him beyond the review of the op. First, I needed to impress the Pear. I still wanted to get assigned to New York and thought that having paid some dues with a successful initial field tour, I was now in a good position to get an assignment there. The possibility was promising, since Headquarters was in another phase of encouraging officers to move to New York, a still unpopular field choice primarily because of financial considerations. Still, I needed his support to get a job there. Second, as fate would have it, I quickly learned that he had been my former husband's chief at the time my ex developed a relationship—and then a marriage—with his agent. The Pear knew more about the end of my marriage than I did.

The Pear was very polite to me and said I should leave the awful hotel where I was staying and he would arrange for me to stay in one of his safe houses, all of which were named after women. I think I ended up in "Nancy," or so one of my buddies later told me.

He invited me for a drink after work. What could I say?

Of course I would never have told the Pear either of my private objectives, but I did agree to a drink with him to discuss the operation I was working on and how it was progressing. Somehow I had the strange instinct to tell him that I had a dinner appointment at eight o'clock with old friends. I didn't, in fact, have any such plan, nor even any particular contacts in New York at the time.

He couldn't have been more charming. And I was impressed with him not only because he was the New York chief, but also because he had served in some exciting foreign assignments and had quite an outstanding operational background of his own. It was easy to ask him about his career and about working in New York. The conversation was going well and he seemed well disposed toward me.

Suddenly he looked at his watch and said we must hurry. I looked at my watch and saw it was only six-thirty and thought to myself that that left an hour and a half till I had to meet "my friends." Hmm. Somewhat uncomfortably, I ordered another drink, thinking to stall our departure and to get a little closer to the eight o'clock hour. I now sensed that he had some ulterior motives of his own, but it was only a guess.

Though I hadn't finished my drink, he ordered a taxi, and we were leaving, regardless of my efforts to delay. He said he wanted to show me one of our special offices. When we got to the location, I jokingly said, "What are we going to do there, ride up and down in the elevator." He replied, "Oh, you're one of those." Gasp. Now I was sure he had a sexual encounter in mind, and he even thought I was kinky, judging from his response to my pathetic but harmless remark about riding the elevators. Sex in an elevator in New York with a senior colleague. No, that was not on my mind.

I couldn't see any way out of this mess without abandoning my New York career plans, though I was beginning to think it would be difficult to work in his office anyway.

When we got to the "special office," the Pear wasted no time. He began to undress. I think he started with his pants, but I can no longer remember exactly how far he got since I quickly left the room, pleading that I had to go to the bathroom. It was my only excuse. He then got on the phone to an apparent aide or colleague and said he was at the "special office with someone." The tone in his voice gave away his intentions to the caller. So now I was not only concerned about getting out of there politely, but I was embarrassed as well. At no time did I think to get mad at him or to say something like, "You disgusting pig." No, I focused my attentions on what I could do to distract him from his immediate goal. I went into the bathroom, took out my red lipstick, and wrote him a message on the mirror. This is not something I would do when visiting anyone else's home, nor would I do it in my own home, but desperation produces rude behavior. He asked what I was doing. I told him to come and see.

He gathered himself together, wandered over to me, and looked at the bathroom mirror. Aghast, he asked what in the world I was doing. He took some small comfort in the flattering note about how "good" he was that I had written to him on the medicine cabinet. Then we began to clean the mirror. I had managed the time well, if not the relationship.

Our time together was running out, thank heavens, and the Pear had lost his inspiration. I had twenty minutes to get to my "meeting" on Forty-Second Street, an address I chose knowing nothing of the area. So we hustled off to a taxi. He delivered me to the place I had indicated, which, unfortunately, appeared to be a shabby diner. Looking somewhat quizzical, he left me there. I went in, waited about a half an hour, and then went back to "Nancy."

By now, I guessed that New York would, once again, not be in my immediate future. I wasn't sure I could handle the work situation on an extended basis anyway, since I had used up most of my wits on this single venture.

After all was said and done, I had managed to introduce the individual of interest to my New York colleague, and the meetings had gone well. On top of it, I made it through the entire trip without totally alienating any of the key men in my immediate professional life—namely the New York chief and the contact, or my own chief back in San Francisco. Whether I had impressed even one of them with my successful professional endeavor was questionable, even though the operation was a success.

I returned to San Francisco, New York no longer in my near future. At this juncture, and for one of the few times in my career, I began to think I might be better suited for other work. Maybe "they" were right. A woman could not do the job. My one little business trip to New York had certainly taken some of the wind out of my sails.

I reluctantly and carefully prepared a résumé covering my life since entering the Agency. I wrote what little I could about my classified job and then submitted the résumé through proper channels for approval. I did not want my immediate boss in San Francisco to know of my plans, of course, but I did carefully send my draft through the chain of command.

Eventually it came back to me, approved, and, bare-bones as it was, I sent letters and résumés to a range of "executive search" firms throughout the U.S. It was the only thing I knew to do. Not surprisingly, I received very few responses to my seventy-five or so letters and a bunch of polite form letters indicating lack of interest in me. The only solid response I received was from an executive who said that his daughter had gone to Wellesley, he lived in San Francisco, and that we should meet. It was very kind of him, but I was getting nowhere in my new job search.

So I was now doing well in my actual work—in my meetings and in my reporting. But my two senior managers were clearly not happy with me, and I doubted very much that the New York chief wanted to see much more of me. And my résumés were getting no responses.

CHAPTER FOURTEEN

THE NATURE OF
THE DOMESTIC WORK

While in San Francisco, I had the opportunity to meet privately with a prominent scientist of international renown. I gave him my entire spiel—CIA connection, ███████████████—and after some discussion of the issues, thanked him and started to say goodbye. I had taken good notes, and while the subject matter was over my head, his approved use of a tape recorder ensured that I could get the detail in scientific terms—at least in language good enough to convey to our scientific analysts. I thanked the gentleman and commented how much I admired his work. He in turn thanked me for visiting him and ended the session with the question: "Please remind me once again who you work for?" So much for my concerns that he might react negatively to a CIA interview.

Another scientist I visited asked me to meet him at his residence as he did not want a "CIA agent" to appear in his office. This was always part of the consideration for us. I was pleased to accommodate his plan and meet him at his home. I had not designated my specific area of interest when requesting the meeting, as we tried to avoid that in any telephone—"open line"—communication. When I arrived, I faced an intercom system with a voice telling me to take the funicular up to the residence. I complied.

Disembarking the funicular, I was invited into the house by a pleasant man who seemed nonthreatening. We sat down in his den, and he immediately asked me whether I had wanted to get together because of the "visiting foreign scientist or the UFOs."

Hmm, he had given me two choices, and the UFO one was enticing, though of course that was not why I was there.

The man had a distinguished background, and I told him that my interest was foreign/international, not intergalactic. We then turned to a useful discussion of the work of his visiting scientist and his assessment of the state of the art of the foreigner's work.

I thanked him for his insightful remarks and prepared to leave. He asked me if I had had any UFO experiences. He explained that he worked with individuals who had been abducted by UFOs but had no recall of their incidents, as UFO experiences tended to be amnesic. I couldn't resist asking if the aliens encountered had six fingers, large thumbs, and little green bodies—after all, my introduction to the CIA had held reference to the little green bodies. He announced that he suspected I had been abducted by a UFO, and asked if I would be willing to remember the experience using hypnosis. I said no.

We parted with his kind offer to assist me if I wanted to learn more about my experience. I declined his offer, noting that it really wouldn't be appropriate for a CIA officer to be hypnotized, much less in order to identify a forgotten UFO abduction.

I also had to debate just how much to report of my meeting when I returned to the office. I knew my male colleagues would enjoy my tale, but suspected the bosses would use it as just one more reason why a female case officer could only get into trouble. My buddies did enjoy the story, and I left it with them. I went on to new projects and never did follow up on my UFO experience. But I've often wondered . . .

Another professor—this one in the most theoretical scientific field—invited me to his office at my request for an initial meeting to discuss certain Russian scientific developments. I was pleased to secure the meeting, since the scientist was both well connected and highly respected in his field. His initial positive response to my invitation boded well, suggesting that I might obtain some useful information on Soviet work in his very specific field, a high-technology area with the potential for military applications.

In this case, the man was comfortable having me in his office. When I arrived, I noticed that his was a little more exotic than the austere atmosphere I was accustomed to finding in the normal academic's office. It had a sort of Bedouin layout, though his desk and work area were clearly separated. He immediately pulled out a beaker and offered me a Bloody Mary. It was eleven in the morning, but I could see he was prepared for all situations. I turned down the drink and somehow got onto the subject of interest, but must admit that I never felt truly in control of the conversation, a key element for a case officer in any professional situation. After our discussion, the scientist walked me out of his office into the open grounds of the building and then leaned over to kiss me goodbye, romantically. I was startled, and probably immediately asked what his wife would think—I had enough data on him to know that he had a family in addition to an outstanding career. He barely drew a breath and looked at me as if I were crazy. Somehow I turned away— politely, I think. I knew I wasn't likely to see this man again. But I've never ceased to be amazed at how some married men are not, as my boss had said, "fanatical about marriage".

Here too I was loath to return to my office and admit that I came back empty-handed. This kind of meeting was exactly what my two bosses anticipated, and here was direct evidence that they were right. So I did not report the outcome of the meeting to my chief when I went back, but merely stated that I had been disappointed in his substantive response. If he'd had truly valuable information, I would have had the integrity to recommend that someone else handle him, but I determined from my meeting with him that his access was in fact limited.

Along with some of these strange encounters, there were moments of success and times when I could feel a sense of genuine contribution. Some of the people I met professionally provided unique and valuable information, material that still remains classified, both in substance and in terms of the individual's access. And sometimes I would get the rare feedback that my report had made it to the White House. That was very exciting.

For the most part, the people I met and interviewed were cooperative and informative. In spite of some of the more colorful moments, the most difficult part of my job now was to educate myself to the point that I could be an effective interlocutor with individuals with outstanding knowledge and expertise well beyond my own. But I always advised that I was not an expert in their field, and that I wanted their advice and commentary for submission to individuals who had appropriate expertise, if not the reputation or renown of some of my contacts.

CALL-INS

One of the assignments all us officers shared was to serve as "duty officer." This can have a lot of different meanings, but in our office it meant weekly or biweekly coverage of the "listed line." In those days the domestic CIA office in a U.S. city would have a listed phone line, which allowed anyone with information of possible value to look up the CIA in the phone book, telephone us, and talk with an intelligence officer.

While most call-ins do not in fact have information of intelligence value, there are definitely occasions when a piece of information or access to such can be extremely valuable. Everyone has read about the handful of cases where a Soviet or other Denied Area diplomat has called a CIA line requesting a meeting. Certainly today, those handling the telephones are always alert to the possibility of a terrorist call-in or alert. No officer wants to miss an important call— or to mis-assess a call-in.

For the most part, however, call-ins provide information of little or no value. Initially I was excited about the listed line duty since so many unusual calls came in, especially in the San Francisco area. If a call came in regarding a particular domestic issue, we would always refer it to the FBI. If it covered any subject that was not of intelligence value, we suggested they call the local newspaper or select civic organizations. As I took more and more of them, I realized that we, the FBI, and the local newspapers had a coterie of odd followers, who would call one of us, get referred to the other, and on and on in circular rotation.

I had two that I came to look on with humor and a certain attachment. They were typical of the kind of calls we got in San Francisco, more typical, regrettably, than the truly valuable intelligence lead.

One Monday, I took a call from a stern-sounding man who wanted to speak to the "agent in charge." Though this was not the CIA's terminology for the duty officer, I said I was the agent in charge. He said, "But you're a woman." I responded with an assertive *yes* and asked what he was calling about. Then he said he was relieved to be speaking to a woman, noting that he was afraid of men anyway. I quickly realized that this was not going to be my golden nugget, but I now felt a certain responsibility to speak with this fellow. He explained that he was in a state hospital and that he had information of great interest to the U.S. government. He asked if I could arrange for him to meet Jackie Kennedy, as he was destined to marry her, at which time he would make certain that I would become the most highly paid agent in the world. After talking for a few minutes, I felt some empathy for this fellow, and we pleasantly ended our conversation, with me making a no promises–style response I developed over time.

The following Monday, I received another urgent call from the same man. Soon I detected a pattern. He had determined that he would get me if he called on Mondays. So he and I agreed that I would be called "Agent Monday". And he called me thereafter with some consistency on my duty days. We developed a pleasant little phone friendship. My grandfather had been a psychiatrist so I was happy to practice what I had learned from him in my new mission.

It was good that I now had an alias to use for my duty days since I wanted each caller to have a sense that they were talking to a real person, but I certainly did not want my name out in public in a way affiliated with the CIA. Now known as "Agent Monday," I developed a minor following of very strange individuals who made a habit of calling on Mondays.

In addition to my telephone pal, I received weekly calls from an unusual woman, whose voice I soon came to recognize. I had a personal rule that I would hear anyone out once, with the view that one should always explore the reason for the call in case there was any intelligence value or national security element in it. But, like my gentleman caller, this woman did not have any information of intelligence value to report.

The first time she called, she requested an in-person meeting. I asked for some details of why she was calling, but hinted that, because it was an open line, I understood that she would need to be discreet. She then proceeded to tell me that she was involved in intergalactic politics. Oops. This did not sound promising. She went on to say, in an utterly sane voice, that she would be moving into space for several months, working on her political scenario, and would contact me when she returned with "very important information." I did not give her the encouragement I had given my gentleman caller, and I tried to point out that we did not have any interest in intergalactic matters. She did not in fact wait several months to call me again, but called every week. That's how I learned the trick of suggesting that she call another agency, since we could not help her. I quickly realized that the FBI and newspapers were sending call-ins to us on the same basis. Some people you simply could not get off the phone, and referring the call helped to end the conversation. I didn't mind her calls so much anyway, since she always ended them by saying

"God bless you," a much more generous phrase than I received from some others.

CHAPTER FIFTEEN

A CASE GONE WRONG

During the late 1970s, the U.S. and the USSR were very much at the height of the Cold War. This meant that we were trying to keep up on every development in the USSR of any possible intelligence value. The human intelligence (HUMINT) part of the business required us to continue to develop human sources. During this time, I began to notice that some of the Soviets, particularly diplomats from the Washington area, would travel to California, a much-loved tourist site, to visit some of the spas in the area. I began to hear of Soviets visiting the "hot tubs" in Big Sur. This of course referred to the hot tubs and some of the human potential programs popular on the West Coast. While I suspected that any Soviet officials would look askance at the idea of going to these sites, it was nonetheless happening.

The Soviet presence in the U.S. was specifically the turf of the FBI and because it was such a large and significant target, we tried to work with them during these early days of cooperation. During the J. Edgar Hoover period, it was well understood that the CIA and the FBI did not work together, coordinate, or even fraternize. But times were changing, slowly, admittedly, but coordination with the FBI was beginning.

So I tried to identify individuals who might seek access to this facet of California culture. It was controversial, since most of my management viewed this cultural sector as "flaky" and as too close to the liberal fringe to be trustworthy, much less informative.

Nonetheless, coordinating with my management, I began to identify some individuals with access ███████████████ ██ ██ ███████████████████████.

Eventually, I found someone with connections to both the Soviets and this particular community. I coordinated with an FBI colleague and eventually met the new individual, explained whom I worked for, and indicated an interest in him. He did not have a negative response to my approach. He was not slamming the door in my face. I still had to assess him, that is, determine his amenability to continuing contact as well as his actual access. A key issue as I got to know him better was his reliability. But we did not use extensive testing to vet U.S. citizens and relied mostly our own assessment of their character and access. ███████████████████ ██ ██ ██████████████████████████.

Over the next few years, I saw this man infrequently but consistently. ██████████████████████████████████ ██ █████████████. I could not fully identify his access, but I knew he was seeing Soviets. ██████████████████████████ ████████████████████████████████. I did not find any negative information on my him and so continued in the relationship. Over the years, he never gave me any single out-standing piece of information, but he was able to provide assess-ments 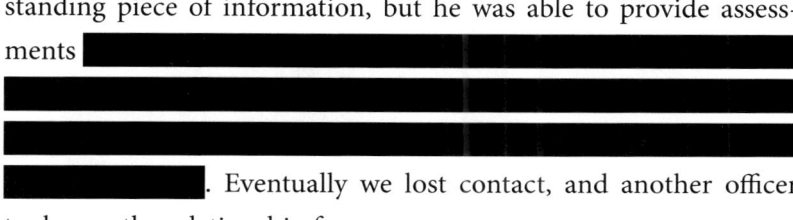. Eventually we lost contact, and another officer took over the relationship from me.

Some years later, when I was serving in New York, I was called on a Friday afternoon and told to report to Washington Monday morning "for a meeting" about a "problem" case. Of course this alarmed me. I contacted a colleague in my chain and over a secure telephone line queried what the meeting was about. I asked if it had anything to do with Mr. X, my old San Francisco case. She confirmed that it did. Somehow, of all the business contacts that I had had over the years, this was the one that came to mind, largely because he was something of an anomaly and because I had never convinced myself as to the exact nature and depth of his access.

I arrived in Headquarters on Monday morning to find that two men from the FBI wanted to interview me. Only a security offi-cer from my organization was present, no one from my actual office, in Headquarters or the field. It was very strange.

In short order, they advised that they were indeed interested in Mr. X. We then spent four hours discussing the case, the outcome being that he had "gone bad." Little did I know that they were actu-ally questioning me about my relationship with him, and investigat-ing the possibility that I, too, was somehow connected to the Soviets in a perilous way. Once I determined that they were not so much interested in my observations as in my possible inclinations, I was horrified. I carefully explained that I had originally sought him out specifically because he was one of the few Americans I had met who had a certain kind of direct access. I had never seen or heard anything to indicate that I should not be in touch with him. The long and short of it was that the FBI and I had a very unpleasant discussion. One of the two agents asked if I would take a polygraph test. By then, irritated and upset, I said no. The top agent excused himself from the room to make a call and came back advising me that I should simply tell my security officer if this man ever tried to contact me again.

What seemed so odd at the time was that they had been looking at him for years, but had never coordinated with me regarding any insights I might have had. Instead they viewed me as a potential problem because I'd met with him. My reasons for meeting were well within our professional construct, and I was basically appalled at the tentative conclusions they had reached. I wish I had had the presence of mind at the time to ask why they suspected this fellow, but I didn't.

The incident underlined the need for closer coordination between our two organizations. If there had been reason not to see this individual, it should have been noted to us by the FBI when I did my original searches. Of course, there is always the other side, which is that if there was a question about me, I should not be notified. This is where the CIA ops officer career gets difficult.

Fortunately, in the end they understood that I had not been in any way coopted. It is hard to imagine another career or situation—outside of wartime or the most serious security crises in our country—that would allow such invasion of privacy and assault on the character of an American citizen as this incident did with me. Although I was offended by the interrogation, I understood that they thought they had reason for concern and had to clear it up without giving me any advance knowledge, in case I were on the wrong side. My management went along with the meeting and provided absolutely no backup or support. It was me on my own with the FBI, unaware of the core purpose of the meeting. An ugly situation.

CHAPTER SIXTEEN

A MANAGEMENT JOB
IN THE FIELD

The clock ran out and my tour in San Francisco was up. Had it been a successful career phase? Well, I made it through, I could say that. And I had done some very productive work and obtained some significant intel. I had also done something relatively few women at the time had done or were doing—taken and completed a full field tour. But my future plans were now unclear, since I saw myself returning to Washington—not to another field assignment—and getting lost in the Headquarters bureaucracy.

As fate would have it, I got a good next job and was assigned a management position by an enlightened colleague of my age, the chief of the field office concerned. He wanted to make me his deputy. He said he was willing to "give me a chance," and made it clear that this was his intention. He knew we were pioneering, that making me his number two was very advanced for the time—1980. He appeared to fully support me and said he wanted a strong deputy with ideas. I was thrilled, since it was the first management job I had been offered.

Initially the assignment went well, but I soon realized that he did not actually want a "strong" deputy. When I suggested an idea at a staff meeting or offered another approach, he politely let me know that he would discuss this with me later, indicating that I should not proceed with my thoughts in the meeting. I, in fact, had given some consideration to new ideas and innovation, based on his initial remarks to me. He later told me that I did not have to offer ideas in those meetings. And then I realized, I was to be yet another type of woman, "the office wife," the woman who sits politely, supports the male leader, and shows no individual initiative. I learned that words and actions were different, but as usual, I did not get it at first.

Though mine was a male/female boss/deputy situation, this incident was also a good study in bureaucracy generally. Through the years, I'd had repeated opportunities to observe that those in charge, at least in my line of work, appreciated quiet, unquestioning subordinates. And that is easy to understand. I myself was not comfortable with confrontation or aggressive people, but I also did not want to be one who had no initiative or ideas.

I did not understand the ways of a successful bureaucrat. And now near midcareer, I knew I was not the ideal employee for a bureaucracy, male or female. Being a woman just made it worse, since any female at the time was noticeable. But how did one progress? It was clear to me that hard work—even good work—was not the full answer. I understood that there were unwritten rules, but I just couldn't entirely figure them all out.

By the time I really came to understand all this—in terms of being a female and working in a bureaucracy—I was fairly well into my career and enjoying the substance, meaning, and value of a career in intelligence, if not the trappings. So in the macro, I was a true believer, and I liked the work. Day to day, however, it was getting to me. As a woman, I saw no alternatives. There were still no role models. The one that I had met in China Ops some years earlier had since retired, and there was no one else on the scene who was at her level that I could see.

The few of us who were working as female case officers were charting our own courses, and we had little contact with or awareness of each other because we were so few, and we were scattered throughout the DO, in the U.S. and abroad. We were none too popular either. I had the feeling, though I used denial to deal with it for many years, that the main men just wished we would fade away. And a number of the women I had known early on did, in fact, just go away. They either got married or decided it was not worth it to continue. According to a study of the CTs of 1967, 68 percent of females separated from the Agency well before retirement age, as compared with 37 percent of men. That meant over one third of my original training class.

At one point, my chief actually took vacation, leaving me as acting head of the field office. The poor man deserved a vacation, but management was concerned about leaving me alone running this installation. Business went along well until a challenge appeared within two days of the chief's absence, one that required a decision by the chief. That was now me! I was excited about the prospect and thought I had worked the problem out quite effectively. In fact, I was pleased with the solution I had decided upon. That afternoon, a senior male from Headquarters appeared in my field office. He generously said that he was there to "help me". Management had sent him over because they were concerned that I would be upset by the challenge and would need some senior input and support, which felt more like parental guidance.

This time, I just caved in quietly. The senior was so polite, and really gave the impression of being concerned. And his solution was exactly the same as mine, so the problem was happily resolved. I didn't upset any apple carts by stating that I could handle the problem on my own. It was clear, however, that Headquarters was not comfortable with me in charge. Being "deputy" was fine. Being "chief" was another story. As long as I was in the Headquarters building a management title was fine, but in the field, even "acting chief" was not yet acceptable.

I did have one slight personnel challenge when I was "acting." Our secretary was a fragile young woman of some twenty-three years. She was responsible for preparing the communications for the office, a significant job, technical and isolating, that required a very disciplined person, but one that had few social requirements due its isolation. I was absolutely sure that she was not the ideal candidate for this position, but I did not even touch that topic. She distinguished herself by wearing to the office big pink fluffy shoes that I always identified as bedroom slippers. But we did not have a dress code, and certainly I, as a woman, was not about to be the only person who commented on her "slippers". However, while in charge, I came to see that her work was as questionable as her dress. One day, I was reviewing some of the recent paperwork and noticed a lot of errors in our communications system. In fact, some 258 items that were cited as "in error" by Headquarters Communications. Since I was technically in charge, I had to rectify this.

I was about to learn another lesson: Do not take on a problem of this size. The current chief had obviously not missed it. He was an intelligent man, but he had chosen not to correct it. Before trying to resolve this problem, I should have realized that. Why? Because it was an overwhelming problem and would point to administrative flaws in the office, which would not be attractive to the Headquarters managers. They did not like trouble.

I understand this now, but I did not then. So I began to correct the errors. Headquarters soon saw the number of papers I was resending. They couldn't believe the quantity and wanted to know what was going on. Ultimately, they acknowledged that there had indeed been a problem, and that they expected it to be fixed.

It was clear to me by this point that a conscientious and prompt response to the problem was not what was desired. A slow, no-one-is-noticing procedure should have been set in place, and over a period of months the errors would have been corrected, quietly and methodically. No one's life was at stake.

I had learned by now that most of my senior male managers—and this would probably have been true of females, too, if there had been any—did not want problems. Resolve it quietly and don't make waves was the process.

To make matters worse, I still had to deal with the woman in the pink slippers, who was basically in charge of this 258-error adventure. In the process of identifying the problem I told her I needed to work with her to get it resolved. I said we could do this together and get everything organized in short order. She tried. Briefly.

The next day she came in to see me and said she was desperate, that I must call an ambulance to have her removed from the office. She said that she was under horrific stress and thought she was having a heart attack. I actually don't recall if we ordered an ambulance. I just know that she turned out to be okay. But I was clearly getting too involved in my work! Problem-solving was not in the cards, at least not in this office. I got it! Finally.

Everything gradually got better, and I soon fit into my number two status appropriately. I stopped coming up with ideas and just edited papers and wrote the occasional fitness reports on those under me.

Still we had another little incident along the way, another learning experience for me. One day, a very attractive young woman who worked for us came back from a meeting and reported that the man—in another U.S. government office—she had met with had asked her if he could tell people she was "his girlfriend," as opposed to stating her true professional affiliation. She seemed very amused by this and returned to her desk, where she repainted her fingernails. We both understood that her contact had not wanted to appear to be in professional touch with our organization, and he had invented the girlfriend line to obfuscate the reason for her presence in his office. Not a great choice, but times were on the verge of change.

The next day, several of the men reported this story back to me as a harassment case. They—and her fiancé, a senior manager in the CIA at the time—had learned of the incident and were appalled. I was appalled too—at their reaction, not her situation. I didn't like her contact's explanation for the meeting, but we had all had these experiences by this time—and many worse, as well. Plus, we were in an unusual business, and inappropriate "cover" was often created to deal with our meetings. It was not always formal and official. On top of that, she had appeared amused, not upset, at the situation when she initially reported it.

The long and short of it is that I finally saw some men take action on behalf of a woman. A suit was filed against the man in the other U.S. government organization, and he was eventually removed from his job—fired. It was my first direct involvement with a harassment case. As a woman, I was astonished that the men stepped in on this one and took such strong action that another man would lose his job. There were so many places that we all needed the male support, but this one seemed pretty slim. I didn't think that this was where the seniors should be putting their EEO emphasis. Knights in shining armor they were, but the case was specious and not deserving of the attention it received. The female work force faced other more telling and serious problems.

CHAPTER SEVENTEEN

BACK AT HEADQUARTERS

My first deputy chief job in the field was nearing completion. I was pleasantly surprised that I was offered another deputy job, but would return to Headquarters for this assignment. They called it "face time," and insisted that I get back to Headquarters and become more widely known to management.

I ended up working for a well-intentioned and intelligent man whose wife, fortunately, had also gone to Wellesley. We had no problems. He was supportive of my work and never uttered a negative comment or gave any indication that he had a problem with women. It was a comfortable time and job, largely because I was working for a man who was accepting. I could just concentrate on the work and the office and not worry about what impression I was making or which female persona I should adopt—quiet and submissive, full of ideas and innovative, nonthreatening, and so on. The idea of "just be yourself," as was so often quoted to me, was simply out of the question. And on those occasions when I did not give that due consideration to choosing the correct female persona and reverted to assuming that good performance and a basic cooperative spirit would be rewarded, I would get a lesson in the opposite.

Shortly there was to be yet another organizational reorganization. Over the years I was to witness an endless number of these. (In fact, by the end of my career, when I was able to predict the organizational trends and upcoming changes, several friends thought I was prescient, when, in fact, I was simply replaying old themes.) When the reorganization occurred, I was moved around once again, along with everyone else.

I was now in my second deputy position, and it was time for another title, which I hoped the reorganization would bring me. So I sat about hoping to eventually be appointed to a more senior job. Based on my now good reviews and job to date, I concluded that I was the natural successor for a certain position that was about to come up. I had received consistently good performance reviews and was getting a lot of hallway comments from colleagues about being "the first woman to . . .". Of course I didn't want to appear too aggressive, so I awaited this new appointment in my semi-quiet, hopefully professional persona. But as I heard more and more about the reorganization, I did not hear my name being mentioned in the rumor mill—RUMINT (rumor intel), as it was known among those of us in the business. Still, I was quite certain I was being considered for something more senior. In fact, I was sure of it.

I finally decided I would informally query the top chief about my next position. Not wanting to be overly direct, I waited for the next encounter with him and rather politely asked when the management jobs would be announced and what I might expect. He inferred, as I had intended, that I might be interested in one of the more senior management positions, one that would be a direct and logical step from my recent field and Headquarters assignments as a deputy.

To my dismay, he registered some surprise that I was interested in these jobs. He said he didn't know I was since I had not said anything. I was shocked, as it was now fairly clear to me that I was absolutely not in the running for the next level. He said I should learn to be direct in such situations. So, I had decided not to be direct, and as a result was not chosen?

Well, not exactly. When I then asked if I should have come to him earlier to tell him of my interest in the next level—even though I had assumed it would be a logical and obvious expectation—he said that he had not even considered me for one of the jobs anyway. I was flabbergasted. I had paid my dues and was, at a minimum, a competent and responsible employee, though my performance reviews certainly indicated a higher level of performance than that. I was seeing a number of male colleagues progress with no more age, skill, experience, or ambition than I thought I had. What could possibly be wrong with me that he had not even considered me for one of the jobs?

By this time I was sufficiently quashed that I could not bring myself to ask why. Cowardly perhaps, but I just did not want to hear any more on that subject at that moment. I had to assimilate what I had just learned. And I had to consider whether I was in fact playing the right role. Was I too direct? Was I too indirect? Just what was going on with my career?

Eventually, I got my new position, a perfectly acceptable one, with the title of Branch Chief. Everything had once again been reorganized, so I wasn't even certain what this title meant. I was about to embark on a series of acting chief positions. These were slightly above deputy chief, but not really potent enough to equate to the actual chief title; rather, I filled in when a chief was absent for some period of time. There were a few women under consideration for such positions, and I was certainly one. I still could not believe, how-ever—and did not accept—that women were not themselves going to get those positions and titles. It was, after all, the early 1980s, not the 50s or 60s.

So I started my new assignment, but as time passed, I began to feel less inspired and less challenged than I had in earlier years. The work was becoming repetitious, though the substance remained important to me.

I persisted, and refocused my energies on getting to New York for my next field assignment. It would still be a feather in my cap, if I could just get there. Unfortunately, by this time a known antiwoman chief was in place there, and there was no immediate hope for a New York assignment, even though it was still a posting that was always understaffed. Senior management finally told me that they thought I would eventually get to New York, but I should not consider it under the current New York leadership. They did not specify why, but we understood each other.

In the meantime, I was sent to a course that became known as "the Women's Course." I went with my good friend from training days. She was progressing along with me at about the same speed, but in an overseas career. (We had taken slightly different directions, but were having some similar experiences, except that she was now mar-ried and fighting issues relating to being a married career woman.) The course was taught by two remarkable women from the West Coast who were advocates of new-wave thinking, which include feminism, among other modern philosophies. I was surprised that the Agency, and specifically the DO, was supporting this training, but I was heartened by the open-mindedness and the willingness to modernize.

During the weeklong class, we received all sorts of hints about how to work with men, emphasizing the lessons learned from the teamwork of sports. We got many tips and heard a lot about mentoring, but we both concluded that neither of us had ever had a mentor. In fact we hardly understood the concept. We also learned about "I owe you" and other little secrets of the male working world—all commonsensical, just only applicable to members of the old boys' club.

One piece of advice given to us was that we should never give away information. In other words, if we had a piece of professional gossip, we should protect it and sell it at the right time; in short, give the information away to the right person at the right moment. Of course, the more useful the info, the more access you would appear to have, and the more valuable your contacts. But, again, I didn't have a lot of professional "club" info.

I soon realized, however, that what little access I had I squandered. I had not understood that information is valuable. In one case, I attended an international conference on terrorism/counterintelligence. At that time, we had been very interested in the responses of key officials of the National Security Council (NSC) to some of our specialized reporting on that subject. I happened to have the opportunity to meet privately with a key NSC official who was the recipient of this reporting. He was enlightened, deeply intelligent, and had been cleared for access to our reporting. We discussed some of the ramifications of my component's reporting, and he expressed his deep gratitude for the substance and quality of what we had been providing. I was very pleased to learn this and was certain that my chief would be happy with my report and my "inside information."

When I returned, my chief asked me about the meetings, and I told him about the meeting with the NSC official and the very positive remarks that he had had on our work and on specific report-ing. But his only response to me: "Was he good?"

As usual I was flabbergasted. I was so certain that he would appreciate my work and my positive and useful feedback, but his only response to my meeting with the NSC official was the sug-gestion that it had been sexual. In the first moment, I did not even understand what he meant, but I quickly got the point. I certainly had learned a good lesson about giving away information. I should have protected it and parceled it out to him amid the proper story of my meeting with the official. I was irritated at the sexual turn of the conversation, particularly since the NSC official and I had had such a meaningful and substantive encounter. But once again, profession-alism was obscured by prurience. It was always disappointing.

In the meantime, I was trying to excel at my branch chief position—or at least to do an acceptable job. I'm not certain there was even room in this job to excel. It was just a time-serving assign-ment, involving a relatively small staff and limited management, but heavy in the frustrations of bureaucracy, complaints about lack of Headquarters responsiveness, and other problems that I never saw corrected in my career years. Too much time was spent on meet-ings; there were too many layers—and none of this would improve in the coming years. Nothing I or anyone else recommended improved things. It was frustrating—not just to me but to all of us in those positions.

During this time, the seniors decided to give me a special assignment. It had no title, but it was a good one. Reagan was presi-dent and was focused on, among other issues, our relationship with Mexico. I was sent around the U.S. to meet every expert on Mexico I could identify and get an appointment with. I did extensive research and pulled out the names of the best people in the field. I set up a series of meetings that necessitated travel throughout the US, and this was definitely exciting to me. All went well until one source contacted an official and said the CIA was approaching Mexico experts and asking a series of national-security-related questions. It wasn't a criticism, but an observation he appropriately felt compelled to pass on. It was true. It was me. So the review came to an end, as it was meant to be off the record, but by then I had collected a serious amount of information and was able to put together a solid paper and briefings.

It was time to visit Mexico for the follow-up and end of the project. My two seniors called me in to the front office and announced that there would be a TDY to Mexico to meet with select individuals, officials, I did not know whom, to review some elements of what I had learned. A trip outside the U.S. at last. My day was coming. I was excited and was by now an expert on the national security aspects of the assignment.

But I was not going on the TDY. No, my two male bosses were, using my studies and information. I rest my case.

CHAPTER EIGHTEEN

BUREAUCRACY

I was beginning to enter a career level where just being a good bureaucrat was a basic requirement. I had now passed the years of new opportunity and the excitement of endless potential, and was in the middle years. While I had had faith in myself as a producer, active, competent, and sometimes innovative, I had no illusions about my skills as a bureaucrat, limited as those requirements were. At this stage of my career, I felt I needed to be a compliant, pleasant individual who worked well within the system. Innovation and outstanding performance (in terms of product) were no longer necessities. Fitting in, however, was.

One very senior officer told me one day, "You are not a bureaucrat." My jaw dropped at the insult, and he quickly said, "That is not bad." And of course, he was right, but I would not know that for a long time to come and in my current status, being a good bureaucrat was what mattered.

So I tried to keep my head down and my ideas to myself. I was less challenged and less hopeful about an exciting future. There were a lot of layers in front of me. Maybe I was not going to advance in the ways I had originally hoped and anticipated. I updated my personal "how to get ahead" profile from "you will get promoted on the quality of your work," to "you will get promoted on your ability to shine as a bureaucrat." I did not associate the word *shine* with *bureaucrat*. I was beginning to run out of roles to play and ideas about which character I should adapt.

Sometime shortly thereafter the New York chief was removed from his position for dereliction of duty. A new chief who was enlightened and accepting of female officers was assigned. Within short order I had a job offer for a managerial position in New York. It was not a fast track to promotion, but I had now placed so many eggs in the New York basket that I was willing to take the job. I wouldn't get promoted for a few years anyway. In the meantime, it was time for my annual performance review. It occurred to me on occasion that the day would come in my life when I would no longer receive a report card, but I wasn't there yet.

My immediate supervisor gave me a good annual report, and I was of course pleased, worrying as I always did about what awful things might be in the report. I did not get that "walk on water" reviews that some of my male colleagues bragged about, but I did get consistently good reviews, with comments about a promising future.

In addition to my immediate supervisor, I received comments—final reviewing comments—from his senior, who was actually a man in our front office. I had to go into the office one Saturday morning to get his review, as it was a quieter time than during the weekdays, and his secretary thought I deserved a few minutes of private time with him.

I sat in his waiting room for quite a while—and I could hear him on the phone, so I knew he was in, but occupied. I had after all read his comments and thought I should just sign the paper and leave. I did this and got up to go home. Just then, he appeared at the door and called me in.

I explained that the comments were all right and that I had signed my concurrence. He asked if I had any questions, and I said I did not particularly like the comment that I needed to "be more decisive," especially since we had discussed that some six months earlier, and I had made a determined effort to improve. This had given me the opportunity to update my earlier role model, which was not to appear too strong, aggressive, or decisive. Now I had a senior boss who was open to the idea of a decisive female, but I did realize that in a continuing effort not to come across as a woman with "sharp elbows," I probably seemed less decisive than I should have.

He said he had seen some progress, but he did not seem convinced. I jumped up and said, "God dammit, you want decisive, I can be decisive." He was appalled. I knew I had been rude, and said I did not think he would like such directness or decisiveness from me. He stood up and closed the door.

Returning to his desk, he admitted, "You have a fine line to walk." He proceeded to tell me that I needed to adopt more of the "personality of a male" in my professional life. He didn't exactly tell me how to do this, and I didn't ask many questions. He went on to say that his wife would have loved to have my job. Well, I thought, I would have loved to have been a wife and a mother . . .

I was now in a really hopeless position, since he was comparing me to his wife, a woman for whom he had true sympathy and who didn't even work. But I was his employee, and I was working. She was his wife and was at home. Was this the competition? It was getting tougher all the time. I now had to add to my portfolio that

I would be getting better opportunities than the wife of the supervisor—most of them did not work in those days. But I was working both because I wanted to and because I had to make a living.

I was finally growing up. At midcareer I realized that I could not overcome these men's concerns about the professional limitations of their wives. Professional performance was becoming less and less of a determiner of my fate. Objective, faceless challenges were confronting me, and I no longer had the answers. There were no role models and no examples. And the obstructions were becoming more abstruse in character but more clear in terms of their insurmountability.

My career was becoming like some middle-aged or midlife marriages. The honeymoon was over and had been for a long time. There were still pluses—substance, patriotism, aspects of a community, a salary. But there were definite minuses now, and no amount of personal or institutional denial obviated them. The system had not made room yet for woman to progress professionally—much beyond the DO's GS-13 level. The female officer was not really respected, and the organization continued to see females in certain defined roles—as reports writers, secretaries, admin assistants and analysts—but not as "on the street" officers. With a few exceptions, the men I knew and worked for did not really see women in the front office, as part of the top management team—much less running a major office or the organization. There were definite societal changes in place, but not yet in the CIA's Directorate of Operations.

One of the most frustrating aspects of this was that so many men I knew and have known over the years tried to be open-minded on the subject of professional women—and thought they were. I cannot recall how many men have said to me that they are supporters of professional women, some even claiming to be "rabid" supporters.

But the truth is that, upon closer examination, it was clear to me that these men surrounded themselves personally and professionally with men, and with women who generally did not challenge their status or their stature. The women who were at their side were often what one might call "yes women." I could always tell how open a man was to professional female progress by the women he associated or aligned himself with. (This is not to be negative about any type of woman. We all have different roles and goals—and only so much time to fulfill any of them, much less all. But it is to say that most of the men I encountered in my professional culture were not attuned to dynamic, professional, feminine/female women who aimed to go to the top, or somewhere near, in their careers.) It wasn't so much that these men were lying as that they didn't actually understand the limitations of their own thinking. They did not and would not acknowledge that they were not making room for female growth.

With my mind still focused on New York and the promise of an assignment there at an appropriate job level, I had a goal and something to look forward to. During this time, though slotted for a specific New York position, I was called to the front office and offered a chief position. Specifically, I was asked if I would take the upcoming job in our Detroit Field Office. The division chief, in offering me this position, said, "You'll be getting what you've always worked for."

This was not exactly what I had been working toward, but that was my secret, and the chief thought it was. That was his agenda, and thus he assumed it was mine. Indeed, I had been offered the number one position in a field installation, but Detroit? If I turned it down, would it reflect to him a lack of ambition? I could not complain about not being given an opportunity to lead. Still single, I did not see myself finding my soul mate, or any other mate, for that matter, in Detroit—it was a city for families, not single people. I said no, but this time the bad was on me. I had turned down a significant assignment, and for my own secret reasons. It was not something to brag about, even to myself.

I heard soon after that a number of men had been offered the slot before me. True or not, I was aware of at least two colleagues who had turned down the Detroit position. One was progressing well in his career anyway, and I rather thought a negative would not harm the others either. Unfortunately a single person, as I was, does not have many excuses to rebuff these positions. I could never imagine saying that I didn't want to go because I was single and worried about having a personal life. One of my colleagues had rejected it because his young child could not get a proper education in Detroit. I could not come up with such an excuse.

Another male colleague and family man repeatedly refused new field assignments, claiming that his wife had health problems. He kept getting promoted from grade to grade through continual reassignment in one field office, where he finally achieved the top position, chief, without ever moving. These excuses worked so well for some. After years in one locale, this same colleague was able to pick off one of the top overseas slots, getting a senior management position in a major European station. His wife must have recovered, because he certainly did not turn down this offer.

I stewed about Detroit, though my heart—and my mind— were not in it. The front office increased the pressure. I was called in by one of the chiefs, not the top one who had offered me "the job that I had always wanted," but his underling, who was senior to me. He tried various lines, such as "You will be the first woman . . . ," and "If you don't take this assignment, another woman will get it" and you will have lost out in the competition. There was, too, the ephemeral promise of promotion. (Oddly, in the DO, unlike the private sector, you can get a job promotion and/or a pay or grade promotion, but one is not necessarily accompanied by the other. Thus, while you may get the chief title, you will be judged for pay or grade promotion at the annual review, when your file is assessed with everyone else's of similar grade and career category.) So a promotion in pay was not a definite in taking the Detroit job, though it was clearly the way management wanted me to go and thus pretty good insurance of that next grade.

I admit all this got to me and to my competitive spirit. But I still knew that others had turned it down, and I tried to dream up an excuse that would let me retain my growing career and still turn the Detroit job down. I decided to hold out for the New York slot, which would be a so-called lateral assignment, but in a key area where our reporting and work really excelled on a fairly frequent basis.

The decision cost me, to the best of my knowledge. I had last been promoted when I was deputy chief in the Washington Field Office. I then did two tours in Headquarters—"Headquarters duty" it was tagged, because it was always viewed as penance/payment for getting a field assignment. And then I would have a few years in New York in two senior management positions. I did not get a promotion in all that time, in spite of continually good fitness reports and prior service in two field installations, as well as Headquarters penance. Was Detroit the only reason?

By this time, I was well aware that there were official files on all personnel and there were "hallway" files. Of course I had no idea what was in my hallway record. I heard many things about myself off and on. One of the rumors I heard with some consistency was that I was wealthy and did not need the money. I was a doctor's daughter, "American royalty," they said, plus I had alimony from my marriage. I could not get rid of the wealthy moniker.

Then I heard from one manager that I might be a "party" girl. It's true that I was divorced and did date—though as I have said, I did have the thought of remarrying, though I had not wanted to advertise that chink in my armor. I blanched when he said "party girl" and have not forgotten it. I can only think that I must have been viewed as quite lively and social because I was involved in a large Gilbert and Sullivan group that put on an annual production in which I sang— on stage—as a chorus member. It was higher profile than the private lives of some of my colleagues, but I was hardly a major performing artist, and I was certainly not involved in anything scandalous.

As for my alimony, I recall chatting with several male colleague of the same grade—and same ambition as I— shortly after my divorce had become final. One of those I felt closest to commented on my solid financial status. He virtually smirked as he said, "You get alimony." I suppose I gasped, but no one noticed those things. In reality, as I've already said, my husband had walked out one day, taken a P.O. box, and left a check for $125 to help me with the ensuing month's mortgage. But I didn't share that information with my colleagues. It was hard enough for me to deal with the tawdry end of my marriage, much less share some of its more disturbing aspects with my office mates. Alimony? No!

CHAPTER NINETEEN

NEW YORK—AND NEW CHALLENGES

I finally moved to New York, by now some twenty years into my career and somewhat long in the tooth for the job, but nonetheless I was excited about the prospect of the substantive work that could be done in this major financial center and international city. There would be opportunities to develop access on a range of national security issues.

I had the good fortune to work for a supportive chief who tried his best to give me every opportunity for growth. He himself said he could not understand why I was not getting promoted, though I had a male colleague who was in a similar position, a man with strong career credentials but glued geographically to New York and thus defined as non-promotable. I had not, however, worked in place. In fact I had moved to several different jobs upon request. So, finally, a good chief, management responsibilities, and excellent substantive work, with the dying days of the Soviet Union and the Gulf tanker wars as major international concerns to be followed.

I still had plenty to learn about working with men, however, and specifically with male managers. I was beginning to get the message quite clearly that they did not like problems. Who did? But there are always a few challenges or areas for improvement in any business situation. In fact, a number of us were beginning to discuss our shared perception that this attitude was true of senior managers in the DO. Denial was a cultural characteristic, as it was in other portions of American society. Oddly, somewhere along the way I had heard that the medics had studied the DO and determined that it was peopled by employees who often came from dysfunctional backgrounds, including families with alcoholism. I opined that it was probably a general male management characteristic that bad news was pretty much unacceptable. For one thing, most managers I knew wanted it to appear that everything under their command was going smoothly. That was certainly understandable, and indeed, in most cases, the trouble spots were hardly enough to bring down a manager or an office, just challenges here and there that needed some fine-tuning.

Early in this tour, however, I was warned that I would be assigned one problem case, not to test my skills, but simply because this employee needed to be assigned somewhere, and I had apparently won the prize.

I saw from the start that she didn't like me. She didn't exactly spit at me, but her body language suggested she would like to. While offering some moral support, my managerial peers told me that she resented my background and thought that I had it easy. I could see immediately that she had a large chip on her shoulder. I sought to win her over and try to make up for all the ugly management experiences she'd had before me. I actually felt bad for her and genuinely wanted to give her a chance for real career growth. In the process, and due to my increasing discomfort in dealing with her confrontational attitude, I adopted a sort of Uriah Heep approach to handling her. She had been bullied by the previous chief, the one who left under something of a cloud. (His management style, aimed at increasing numbers and production levels, was to yell at a less-productive employee across a large room—something like a journalists' pit—telling the delinquent officer to improve his or her performance.) Based on this, I was pretty certain I could help this woman and have her enjoy her tour as well.

I was wrong. I didn't understand that sometimes the one bullied becomes the bully. My increasingly unctuous managerial efforts did not appease her. Nonetheless, I tried. She demonstrated some enthusiasm about her work. But regretfully, I began to notice that her writing and reporting were not very good. Sometimes she would write reports on fast-moving situations that were about to be in the public domain. (We reported only information that could be regarded as intelligence, i.e., never information that was already publicly available.)

One night she called me into the office late in the evening to approve and send something she had just written. I headed there in spite of the hour and was excited at the prospect of what she must have just gotten and prepared for transmission to Washington.

I reviewed her report and saw immediately that the information was already known. I'd seen references to it in the newspaper. I asked her what was new about this information and what in it required alerting the senior DO duty officer in Washington. She insisted it was breaking news. I told her that it was news that had already broken, just, but nonetheless broken. I could not release this information and alert the nighttime management team in Washington that we had this story. It was indeed newsworthy, but it was not intelligence. She and I had quite a debate about it, but I stood firm in refusing to send it in. The last thing the station and the chief needed was to be responsible for sending in material that was already in the public domain.

She was furious and asserted to me that she would never call me in again in the middle of the night. I was concerned about her aggressive response, as I had been in other encounters with her, but I stood my ground, hoping that I had made the correct decision not to embarrass the office or the chief, especially to Headquarters.

Fortunately for me, the story was very much in the news the next morning and indeed would already have been known to Washington. She and I never again discussed the matter, but I was relieved that I had made the right decision not to approve sending in the material, waking up senior managers in the middle of the night, and for the wrong reason.

When I had the unhappy task of writing her annual fitness report, I debated just how direct to be. There was an unwritten rule of thumb that a fitness report generally gave good grades across the board to a good or average performer. The "walk on water" reports went primarily to men who were intended for promotion to the next level, which would allow them to move up the management scale. A negative report, even on a single area of performance, was often viewed as potentially damaging to one's career over not just the immediate tour, but the longer run. This was true because there were so few negatives in a normal annual report that reviewers immediately picked out the best and the worst fitness reports and put them aside—in promotable and non-promotable clusters. The rest fell in the middle and took more serious review and analysis by the presumed objective review panels who choose employees for annual promotion.

I struggled with the report, trying to think how I could possibly put it together in such a way as to prevent an outburst from her and at the same time to retain integrity in what I was writing. Realizing that the reviewer can read between the lines, I wrote of her solid accomplishments but made a fairly benign reference to her need to "continue to work on her skills as a team player."

When she read the report, she was enraged. She responded that it would ruin her career, that I was out to get her, and more. I have to admit that she was intimidating, as I had never encountered an employee, much less my own subordinate, who would throw papers and use four-letter words directed at me.

I considered backing down on my review but also felt a commitment at least to myself to be honest. I had not done her any major harm, and she did need to improve her team skills. She was the subject of a broad range of office complaints and a source of disruption to a number of her colleagues, many of whom spoke to me off the record about her authoritarianism. It was odd, given that I had initially met her as the subject of her former manager's bullying.

I didn't cave in, but I went to the chief and the deputy and said that we needed to discuss this case. The three of us, two men and me, sat down and reviewed the performance. The men were disinclined to include any critical remarks, which meant I would have to edit what was meant to be my honest appraisal of her performance. I said that I would change my review, but I wanted to note to them for the record that I was concerned about her behavior and did not think she was performing as a reliable and responsible case officer. I suggested she had sociopathic tendencies.

To my surprise, both men agreed completely with what I had just said, even with the diagnosis, which I had reached with some help from my wise physician father. But they were pleased to go ahead with the positive review and let her career take whatever course those reports led her to. In the macro, I felt sorry for her, though I did not respect her unprofessional office behavior. I had been wrong about being able to help or advance her and saw overall that she did not like me from the start because of my background and the apparent ease with which she thought I had gotten to my current position.

I have often reflected on this isolated event as I formed the view about the denial attitude of senior male management—in general, not specifically—to difficult cases. Some years later, when Aldrich Ames was finally caught for treason, I watched with agony the organization's process of reviewing his career and his descent. I was disappointed but not shocked that senior managers, many of whom were friends, would say to me that no one was directly responsible and that there were good reasons for letting Ames continue in his career—even though before being caught he appeared to have drinking, family, and career problems. The treason had not yet been identified. (In fairness, there was always a reason for retaining DO employees with personal problems, because it was better to retain them than to anger them and have them leave on bad terms. It was a challenging counterintelligence issue.)

Still, from my perspective, denial was again at work. There was so much unwritten language and talk of hallway reputations, while at the same time a whole process was in place, in terms of annual performance reports and promotions, to ensure a "fair and equitable" process. I got that there is more to an employee than his or her individual file. And I certainly understood that there needed to be a cooperative and positive team in place in each field installation to succeed. But I could not understand the need for denial of truly negative performance or behavior. Nor could I understand the apparent dichotomy between the integrity of the performance review system and annual promotion panels, and the hallway reputation and inside deals done by senior managers to assure certain promotions for preferred individuals.

The human element was understandable, but the system claimed to be fair and objective while offline it assured the growth of some individuals whose annual reviews did not appear greater than others. There were many who were promoted for excellent performance. It is just that there was also a lot of gray area.

The problem with all this for a female case officer was that those getting promoted to the more senior management positions— and thus to the higher pay, grade, and recognition levels—were men. How could one hope to compete fairly in a system that had two differing operating levels—one public and one never stated? A female officer could receive virtually the same fitness report as a male of similar grade, performance, even skills, but the promotion would rarely be awarded, and more important, the career growth would not go to her.

The system was in place. There was nothing to say or do except to assume that the best people were getting promoted. As I grew in career background and years in service, I did not think the system was in fact that fair—fair, but not that fair—but I had absolutely no way to prove it. It would all be a matter of words. There was nowhere to go.

So I languished in grade, listening to rumors that I wanted to be in New York and would never move, and that this would end my career. I should note here that as one falls behind peers in grade, fewer high-level opportunities occur. This is obvious, but was another serious problem for women. For example, if you remained in grade as a GS-13 while your male peers progressed to GS-14, 15, and up, your job opportunities would no longer be equal.

Still, I could not see what was holding me back from getting promoted. My reviews were excellent. I was committed to the system and the organization; some of my reporting was receiving high reviews and was proving influential in terms of policymaking in downtown Washington; and I was managing an effective and productive program.

The DO is unique in its inability to satisfy individual ego needs. In other words, as a DO officer, you can have no public recognition or renown. The only reward for performance is growth internally, both in grade and salary, official recognition, and increased challenge. I do not think that senior management has ever really come to terms with this inherent psychological challenge. It is specific to the Agency and primarily to the DO. The DO tries to attract individuals with a "can-do" attitude, the risk-takers. The lack of attention to the individual ego and its marriage to the unique personality and character traits required of the DO officer have not in my view yet been properly analyzed or understood. Of all systems, this is one where performance should receive more, not less, recognition. The idea that the reward is in just being a DO officer wears thin as the years pass, not early on, but later.

But as I said, my New York chief was incredibly supportive. He was the best I had ever had, and he had a daughter who was beginning what would eventually be a very distinguished career herself as a case officer. I think that made him sympathetic to me. One day he decided to create a new job for me, one that would take me out of the branch chief position, which was fine with me, though I needed the title.

He would make me chief of operations (COPS), a new position in our office and one that was an essential part of every overseas station. It was a job with real cachet in the DO. I was given a superb assistant, and we started reviewing all the sources in our field office who had operational potential. ████████████████████ ██████████████. This meant some coordination with the FBI ██████████████████████████████████████ ████████. I couldn't have been happier or more grateful, promotion or not.

CHAPTER TWENTY

CHIEF OF STATION

During my last year in New York and under the management of a new senior Headquarters chief with broad Agency experience in both the DI and the DO, I was offered a new position, one as Chief of Station (COS) at one of our good domestic sites. I accepted without hesitation and was in fact thrilled to earn the COS title and the new job, even though it would mean leaving New York at the end of the tour.

While a number of people complimented me on this achievement, some said they "and others" were surprised that I had agreed to move. Again, I had to fight the hallway RUMINT. I had only turned down one assignment thus far, to Detroit, some years earlier, in tandem with a number of male colleagues.

Colleagues said my new position would ensure the next promotion. And eventually it did. In the early days of my career, I had not so much cared about growth because the job was so rewarding in itself. But, by midcareer and later, I had the same ambition that my male colleagues did. I wanted to do well and assumed that a good performance would be accompanied by new opportunity and growth. This also meant increased pay—that is, recognition for performance.

There were so many positives, so many good things in place in my career now, including the substantive aspects of the assignment, because I would be overseeing the office collection across all our areas of focus, a range of national security concerns. But in spite of this career development and title, it had been slow real growth. I had been in grade for eight years. Long in the tooth, to say the least. With my new assignment, the cancellation of my renewed New York lease, and my immediate move to another U.S. city, I now had the hope of a challenging new job and serious career growth.

And one that would allow for real management responsibility—in effect, running my own station. But following my transfer and my first months in the COS job, I still had not received a promotion. Instead, when promotions were announced, I was given a routine step increase. While I was pleased to get even a small increase in my finances, with my transfer and new position I was beginning to chafe, even to become embittered at my inability to get promoted. During the past eight to nine years in grade, I had served as deputy in one field installation, followed by two separate managerial assignments in Washington, a special assignment on a Mexican task force, as well as branch chief for oil/energy and political issues, and chief of operations in New York.

Still the new job as Chief of Station proved to be challenging and fulfilling. Substantively, it was ███████████ the Cold War and we were getting some excellent reporting on Communist East Germany, such a hard target that I had rarely in my career had any access to material or assets on that geographical region. To wit, good luck and timing enabled us to find an excellent source with direct

information on East Germany and a sure feeling that ███████████
████████████. █proved right. We were not far ahead of the news on this one, but we still had the story that was a surprise to virtually everyone, and our reporting got to the White House.

I enjoyed having my own office and being able to work with a group of primarily young officers who were enthusiastic about their assignments and about the overall mission of the Agency. As before, our administrative staff was made up largely of women who had long held their jobs in the clerical field in the station. They were the real stalwarts, and they are never fully recompensed for the job they do.

People in those jobs often carry the historical knowledge that can be so critical in our business.

In one such case, my head secretary heard me take a call on our listed line. As always, I checked the office records and files to determine whether this caller was known to us. There was no record of any kind. As I was talking with him, my secretary interrupted me and quietly said she thought this was a problem caller. I asked what she meant. She said she recognized the name and recalled that this man had been put in a special "no contact" status because of a serious security problem with him.

I took her word and completed the call politely, stating I would get back to him soon with some feedback as to interest in what he was calling about. In reviewing the material with Washington, I discovered that this man was involved in litigation concerning a national security issue. I had to recontact him and let him know that we would not be meeting, while appearing to have interest in the subject matter he had called about and not referring to the pending litigation. It was quite clear that he had "hot" information, but the legal concerns precluded our seeing him. The secretary saved the day with her historical recall, even though there was no record in the station.

This kind of situation presents a continual problem for the Agency. Namely, the nature of our contacts and sources. If a person has a questionable background, serious consideration is always given as to whether or not we should be in contact with him. The critical national security concern develops when such a person has information of real value to the U.S. government, yet for litigious or political reasons, we cannot have contact with the individual. ██. While we were not sitting in the midst of the Middle East, our office was able to do some very significant reporting in support of our actions ████ ████. One of the blessings of the presence of American business and economic efforts abroad is that the United States, specifically U.S. business, has played a major role in developing the infrastructure of key countries in the developing world. Since the U.S. built so many of the pipelines, oil infrastructure, and more sensitive infrastructure in some of the key countries in the Middle East, it was possible to approach extremely knowledgeable sources and learn specifics that could affect our national security plans. Indeed, some of the material we and others were able to obtain ████████████████████ ████████ enabled the U.S. ████████████████ to avoid harm in some areas ████████████████████████████.

And so it was an exciting time because the U.S. was involved in critical international activity in both the Persian Gulf and the USSR. ████████████████████████████, more and more Americans or friends of Americans were ████████████████ attaining access to decision-makers, not only in political but in scientific and even military fields.

While my work was extremely gratifying at this point, and while I actually had a title that I had long desired, there continued to be some challenging aspects in the strange male-female culture, even during this period. I had a colleague in another local CIA office who had separate but related responsibilities; that is, he covered the same substantive areas I did, but using a different set of contacts— ███████████████████████████████. We were equals and meant to coordinate our work.

During our tours, the senior management of the Agency in Langley decided to combine our two offices ██████████████ ███████████████████████, a decision I fully supported because I thought it would increase efficiency and coordination, even if there would be some awkward areas of merging.

I had the good fortune to be chosen to take over the new office. This was all handled rather delicately, but the decision was that I would manage the new office with the departure of the other chief the following summer, though I assumed the new title immediately. It was a sensible strategic decision as he was near the end of his assignment.

We two were left to our own devices to work this out together and to eliminate one office, one location, and some personnel, and then coordinate the administration, logistics, and operations of both offices. This turned out to be a major undertaking, starting initially with the appointment of me as the new and only chief.

While I had been flattered to be chosen, the nine-month waiting period for the other chief to depart proved challenging, to say the least, when we set about reducing our facilities to one location, one set of staff, and combining all our operations, with all that that implied. By now I couldn't understand why the senior management in Langley didn't just tell us to wait until the end of the other officer's tour, or just make me chief and commit to that. I would happily have gone with either choice. But once again I witnessed the tendency on the part of the senior leadership to try to appease everyone, while avoiding tough decisions. I eventually learned that my bosses had already had trouble with my colleague, which was one of the reasons I got the job, but they chose to back-burner the problem and just wait until his tour was up and hope he would retire.

Since none of the above happened, we began jointly to work out our moves and plans for consolidation. Two offices in very different parts of the city had to be shut down, and one new location chosen. This meant that some personnel would have to commute further among other things. All in all, a complex set of problems ensuring that not everyone would be happy.

After a promising start, I found that my co-chief was not as amenable to the changes as I had thought from his initial polite and accepting reaction, along the lines of "I'm glad you're getting the new office. I want to leave anyway, have had enough . . ." By this stage in my career and life, I was not so naive as to believe that he was one hundred percent behind those words, but I basically thought that he was pretty pleased to be moving on. Wrong.

The first meeting we had to coordinate our offices, he came equipped with information that one of my employees had lied about some of the logistics in the office, something that would have been important to the new office, not to mention the ethical seriousness of the complaint. I had to get to the bottom of the accusation, while not accusing my employee of any inappropriate action or appearing to take my counterpart's allegation seriously.

After some examination of the issue, I concluded that my co-chief had laid the first roadblock in our transition. My subordinate hadn't lied and I knew it. The retiring chief was never able to produce any evidence of wrongdoing and eventually caved in on his criticisms. One challenge met, but a little bloodshed nonetheless. The warning flag had been waved, and he was going to make the transition difficult, but not in any way that could be discussed elsewhere without making it appear that I was not up to handling the situation. I was stuck.

In the meantime, Washington continued to ask for updates on how our consolidation was coming along. The school answer to this was—Fine. They wanted the consolidation to occur and without any problems, but they didn't provide backup. As so often happens, they didn't want to hear any bad news and, in another case of "no flies on me," didn't want to make any tough decisions.

For his next act, my colleague chief called me over to his old office for a meeting with his remaining staff to discuss the consolidation. When I appeared, he invited me in, calling me "Honey," to meet his entire staff. He opened the meeting, said I would talk about the transition, and promptly left for the day. It was not closing time, but he had a statement to make and he made it. He wasn't going to sit for this transition with me in charge and give his support to the changes. He would walk out.

By now I no longer took any of his actions seriously and understood that the consolidation would happen on my watch with help from my immediate employees, but none from him.

When the whole matter was over, we had a good and workable new office. Everything had changed, but the younger officers in my station said they still couldn't believe I let him call me "Honey" all the time. I said it was a better epithet than the other options. I had worked longer than they had in a world where men like this one would not be managed by a woman. I knew he wasn't going to change. I could live with "Honey" if it was the least of my problems with him, but it didn't win me any points with my younger staff.

We all moved on. I assumed my colleague had gone on to retirement as both rumored and reported. But I later ran into him in the halls of Langley, only to learn that he had taken an overseas assignment. Things were never quite as they should be, but he had been a good operations officer, if not a good manager, so perhaps he continued to serve well.

By this time there were two of us—women, that is—who attended the annual COS meetings for our division, which consisted of some ██████████ colleagues of similar rank. We were both aware that a certain number of eyes were on us—to see if we would have catfights or get along. Since we were already great friends, we got along. We sometimes took long walks while at the COS meeting at the Farm. And sometimes we would get comments about our walks when we returned: What did you talk about?

There is no question that progress for women in the DO was occurring, and indeed the younger men, the younger chiefs, were supportive and socialized extensively with us during the meeting. Some of the older fellows—namely, those of my age group—kept more to themselves and didn't spend much time developing their relationships with either of us, beyond what already existed. Nonetheless, times were changing. It was the early 1990s, and I could feel a distinct difference in the views toward and treatment of women professionals. At least I heard less negative talk than in earlier days.

In one amusing moment at a Farm COS training session, the instructors did a little exercise with us that included dividing the room into those who watched television and those who didn't. While I had, in my earlier days, not watched television on a regular basis, I did at this stage of my life turn it on every morning while I was dressing for work. I decided to be honest about my TV orientation and promptly went to the side of the room for the TV watchers. To my surprise, I was almost alone in the group. I didn't particularly want to look as if I spent my life tuned in to nightly sitcoms or whatever, but I was really surprised that I was one of the few who watched TV. Hmm.

During class breaks the next day, I noticed that most of the guys were sitting around the television in the main room and watching avidly. I was not. This did not exactly fit with the image they'd presented the day before. Later in the afternoon, I jokingly queried a few friends about this—only to hear that they "were not watching TV." Well, then what were they doing? I asked. One responded that they were "watching sports." Now I got it! Watching sports did not mean watching TV. Hours in front of the TV focusing on football did not count. Another small epiphany.

I was getting there, slowly but surely. In spite of having grown up with brothers, I was not learning fast about the male mentality in the workplace. It really was different. What I began to suspect over time is that the old adage that women are complex should have been applied to men. They really do speak different languages socially, with women, and professionally (and probably in the locker room, but I haven't spent much time there). Men, I decided, were complex creatures with sets of unwritten rules and guidelines that you could only guess at if you were an uninformed women. There really was a "men's club," and even if some men were not on the A team, they were still members. Females were not.

I returned from training and the annual COS conference to my station and began to plan my next career move. By this time, I knew I needed to go back to Washington to a Headquarters assignment in order to continue a proper career progression; more face time was required. But, I had finally gotten to the field and now wanted to spend more time away from Headquarters. I had already paid my dues, having spent more than half of my career in the D.C. area, serving in field support jobs.

This logic did not impress the seniors at home. They insisted that I take my next assignment in Washington and try to get the next titled position, one that would allow me to be considered for the next promotion. As I've noted, there was never a promise of promotion, merely placement in a proper position (slot), management support, and the hope of the next promotion if you did well in the new assignment.

I was once again eager to get overseas. I had served in a number of domestic assignments, and having started my career in search of an overseas assignment, I wanted to take another shot at it. I had a good background and considerable experience in a variety of intelligence modes. Further, times had changed; there were a number of female case officers overseas now.

So I put all my eggs in one basket—a specific overseas assignment, mind you, one for which I was well qualified and a true candidate, was coming up, and I wanted it. But that would mean accepting a transfer at my same grade, no promotion in sight.

Well, I had never received a promotion directly with any move, physical or titled, at any point in my career. Unlike the private sector, the DO can award you a new assignment and the hope of a promotion, but, as I noted earlier, the promotion comes separately. It is an odd approach, but one fully accepted in our system. One might argue that the actual promotion should accompany the job promotion, move, or new title. This was not the way of the DO, and I knew that.

The overseas position I wanted was specific to the work I had been doing and something the new Headquarters chief, with DI background, had come up with. I had the perfect qualifications. I discussed it with him and he assured me it would be my next assignment. In effect, he promised me. To be honest, the overseas slot meant more to me than a promotion, though I didn't advertise that.

Time passed, and I heard no further word from the Washington managers but wanted to begin language studies. So I began to ask about the status of this assignment. Most of the men I was in contact with were by now old colleagues and friends. But I noticed they stopped returning my calls. Finally, my communications officer came to me one day with a personnel cable she wanted to bring to my immediate attention.

I read it with consternation. It simply stated that I should return to Washington for my next assignment. It went on to say directly that another officer had been chosen for overseas.

After almost a year of effort and waiting, I had been turned down. Several of my supporters called to let me know they had had nothing to do with it but they were surprised I didn't get it. I wondered if I had also shot myself in the foot by lobbying so hard for the slot.

By demonstrating my interest in a lateral transfer to an overseas slot, I had revealed that raw ambition was not my sole aim. I had let it be known that there were other things than a promotion or a title that could appease me and fulfill my needs.

In addition, and perhaps more important, I was angered at the lack of candor in their earlier support of my application for this job, which they must have known would go to another many months earlier. I could have readjusted my career plans and aims if they had been honest and direct enough to tell me that they were considering me for other jobs and that the overseas slot was not going to be given to me. Instead I had held on for almost a year, passing up other opportunities—namely, openings that one had to apply for in the forthcoming year.

I did advise one colleague in the decision-making chain that I was very disappointed, and that I would have appreciated their dealing directly with me, after all these years, instead of sending me a cable advising me of a decision that had been made months earlier, though not on paper. They could have called me. We had after all worked together for some twenty years. Though a longtime career friend, he said my attitude was not helpful. He also intimated that I was not being a "team player" in this particular case. He was right. I wasn't a team player on this matter. I felt I'd been led on and now was left in a position where the key jobs for the upcoming term had already been filled. I had not applied for any, thinking that I had my ace in the hole.

Perhaps most important in that moment, my own staff of young officers picked up that I was upset and concluded that I had been put aside and abused by management. This was not exactly the case, though I had ultimately limited myself to a single goal. But several of my young female officers said they were beginning to wonder about their own career futures in the organization, whether they would be treated honestly and fairly. I argued that my case, in this particular instance, was anomalous. I really did not think it applied to them. They saw and knew that I had been playing a waiting game—and they surmised as well that I had been kept on the hook and not dealt with directly in spite of my years of experience. They also saw that I was not going on to the next management job, but they did not fully understand that I had played a key role in making this immediate determination. I tried to explain that, in spite of my personal disappointment, the overseas posting had not been the best career move for me anyway, and that I had not been treated unfairly in terms of being overlooked for the next career growth step.

I settled down and adjusted to the disappointment. Soon thereafter, and with some trepidation, I headed to Washington to meet with a new senior manager to discuss my next assignment. I was ready for change, and this particular man fully understood and supported that.

When I arrived in Headquarters for the meeting, I was actually quite nervous. I hadn't seen any of these colleagues since the overseas decision. and I was a bit uncertain about my standing. The new boss, a career professional from the DI, a more enlightened component of the CIA with regard to women, was both generous and respectful of my career contributions. To my pleasant surprise, he asked me what assignment I would like among those few now left and said he would do what he could to accommodate me and try to find a higher slot for me. By this time, I had already served in one way or another in most of the remaining positions, and though I appreciated his support, I could not identify one that would be motivating or hold new challenges.

CHAPTER TWENTY-ONE

CONGRESSIONAL AFFAIRS— AND THE SEVENTH FLOOR

I told the chief I needed a change and new challenges. He said he knew of a position outside of the DO, in the Office of Congressional Affairs (OCA), in the Office of the Director of the CIA (DCI), that I might apply for. He said he would give me his support for this job.

There are differing opinions on serving outside of the DO club. One school says that in order to progress to the higher grades in the service, the officer must work at least once outside the officer's career silo, particularly if the person has always served only in the DO. This became known as an "out-of-body" experience, touted by many at the senior levels as essential to senior growth in the organization.

The other view, and the one that became true for me, was that you should continue to have face time among the decision-makers in your own directorate. This meant taking the next higher position one could get within the DO.

Nothing was certain regarding promotions, so I interviewed with OCA for a job on the esteemed "Seventh Floor" which held the Director's staff and office. I learned I was being considered for a senior position at a higher grade than I was actually in. I was excited. This might in fact give me an opportunity to do a challenging job while having the chance to get promoted, even though outside my own career silo for a period of time. I had heard throughout my career that the DO was the slowest with promotions—the honor of serving was always considered part of the reward. But I didn't realize the truth of this until now, when I was being considered for a job in the OCA at a seriously higher grade than my current level and one that would have presented exciting challenges.

Of course, well over twenty years into my career, there were a number of colleagues of the same age and time in as I, senior peer males now higher in grade than I was, who were also interviewing for the job. After being held under consideration for about ten days, I was told that while I had made the top three, another had been chosen, one who outranked me gradewise. I was disappointed, but I understood that I had been dealt with fairly and taken seriously.

The man who got the job was at least three grades ahead of me and ready for a new assignment, and without question he was excellent. I understood that, regardless of my record, I really had no chance in that competition. But I would still suffer from legitimate competition with similarly aged male officers who really were senior to me in grade due to years of growth and promotion. I could never have achieved their grade level during my career because of the absence of opportunity for females along the way. Now I was paying the price just for not having been competitive through the years. In other words, it could have been a fair competition at this point, but I was barely in the running.

I was flattered that I had been treated with fairness by OCA management and actually considered for the job. They said that while they could not offer me the original job, they would like to have me come to OCA in a lateral position since they had a slot available. I was ready for the change and thought the chance to work in the DCI area with Congress could prove fascinating.

In addition, I would have an out-of-body experience (out of the DO) and expand my career portfolio. I was now in precisely the same position, promotion wise, as I had been in a year earlier when I had let it be known that I would take the overseas assignment, even though lateral. So, a year-plus later, I would get a new job, in Headquarters, at my current grade level, without promotion in sight. What had happened to my growth?

OCA had its own set of challenges, ones not relating to gender at all; rather to being on the seventh floor and among the most ambitious bureaucrats in the organization. Overall I had a good experience there, a time unlike any other I had seen throughout my career. Spending time on Capitol Hill in endless briefings on substantive issues was its own reward. On the seventh floor, I did, however, meet some of the nastiest colleagues I was to come across in my career. There were continual turf battles, though never in the open. As I said before, I was not a particularly outstanding bureaucrat, but if I learned anything on that floor, it was to keep your cards close to your own chest and not cross anyone—with ideas, talent, or challenge. The old expression that it's best to hide in the tall grass was certainly true in the DCI's area.

At one point, I was called in by my immediate boss, another senior male, who asked me "on behalf of his supervisor" if I was "trying to get discovered". Apparently I had spent too much time trying to get memos signed off by the assistants to the DCI. Since I was getting late in my career and was already over fifty years old, I found my supervisor's question both strange and insulting. By now, I'd been around some twenty-five years. It was a little late in the game to be a chorus girl. I was offended by the remarks because I had been working tremendously long hours, trying to meet deadlines that were virtually impossible to meet. I was frequently wandering the seventh floor after normal work hours, looking for a senior officer to sign off on a paper for Capitol Hill.

At times I was amazed we ever met any deadlines, given the number of signatures required and the number of changes made to various papers, before finalization and DCI sign-off. I continued to be surprised at the resistance to change or innovation. Although I had witnessed that resistance throughout my DO career, I saw it even more clearly when I was on the seventh floor. For example, a couple of colleagues and I developed the idea of a small "outreach" program to the new Congress—the Newt Gingrich Congress, as I called it. It was the most basic idea—initiate contact with formerly unseen members of Congress and advise them that OCA can provide them briefings on key international and intelligence topics.

Amazingly, I began to hear hallway references to the O word. The outreach idea was considered by many to be too aggressive and outward oriented. It would have to be developed slowly. Well, I knew that it would move slowly in any case, since that is the way in a bureaucracy—except in wartime or the most critical situations, when decisions can be made very rapidly. But I was surprised that the program seemed threatening to some individuals. No information would be inappropriately revealed to Congress, and we already had extensive oversight. Why not take a positive approach to Congress instead of always being reactive?

I knew the program was doomed when my immediate boss stopped me in the hall and casually asked if I had heard that the outreach program had been "stabbed in the back." It was such a strange and intense question. Of course I hadn't heard a word, but I saw the writing on the wall. How could I not? The old managers were not going to have a real outreach program. I was too low on the food chain to effect changes.

My outreach ideas mutated from an initial effort to expand our congressional contacts into a program that oversaw the congressional travel schedule for members or staffers who wished to visit CIA installations outside of Washington, in the U.S. and abroad.

As one always finds when coming to a new office, I was initially assigned the less-than-hot jobs. In other words, I was only occasionally working with our oversight committees in spite of the fact that I was one of the few DO officers in OCA. While my boss continued to say that I would "eventually" be given more responsibility with those committees—a step that would have greatly enhanced my promotability within the DO—this was just not going to happen. My whole DO experience was virtually put aside while I was in OCA, only to be handled by others who liked the excitement of the job but did not have the DO background.

I had another unfortunate episode with this particular boss. I had set up a briefing with a significant member of Congress, one whom I had in fact already met in a previous briefing when I accompanied the DI analyst. When the then chief of OCA heard of the new meeting, he insisted I be accompanied by a senior male officer, in fact, the boss who had warned me about my outreach efforts. So we headed to the Hill together for the session, with our expert briefer from the DI. When we got to the congressman's office, he welcomed me in, having already met me, and asked my superior male colleague to remain in the hallway until the briefing was finished. It was a deeply embarrassing moment, but my boss and I never discussed it. He just sat on the hallway chair waiting for us to emerge.

Amid all of this, I set out—with approval, of course—to make some new congressional contacts. I called one congressman who was known to my family because of some property we owned in his district. I went to see him and was pleased at his receptivity. He had an intelligence background and was amenable to appropriate contact. He even said I could use his office, if necessary, when I was on the Hill.

I reported this very positive meeting back to my seniors. The chief of OCA later asked me why I was wasting my time "on those Republicans." I embarrassedly replied that I was only hoping to expand the contacts on behalf of our organization.

As fate would have it, the next Congress turned out to be Republican. And the most significant congressional person currently handling the Congressional Oversight Committee was the very member with whom I had initiated contact. He eventually became DCI. And that had all started with my outreach to him. It had not turned out to be a waste after all.

By this time, I was beginning to think very seriously about retirement and getting into the private sector for at least some part of my career life. It had now been well over two decades for me and it was time. I had given up on the overseas assignments though I knew that I would always regret that I had not had them. And OCA had been so interesting that I began to consider other kinds of work with the Agency and the Intelligence Community. There were other places to play a role, and some of my advisers had been right in telling me earlier that I needed some work experience outside of the DO.

I learned more in my several years in OCA about my business, the U.S. Congress, lawmaking, the US government, and the Intelligence Community than I had learned at any other time. The

OCA job was an eye-opener and an education. It gave me a lot of insight as well into the harsh and competitive politics of the seventh floor.

When I finally left OCA at the end of my assignment, the chief—yet another new one from outside—offered me one of the best compliments I had had in my entire career: he asked me to extend my service in OCA, but his words were ones I had waited my whole work life to hear—"You are exactly the kind of person needed in this job."

CHAPTER TWENTY-TWO

WOMEN'S PROGRESS

By the early 1990s, women were still on a desperately slow growth curve in the DO, and there were still few significant role models. Most important, there were no known keys to success. Of course this was true for men as well, but at least there were abundant examples of successful men in the DO to emulate, and it was fairly clear how they got ahead. Women continued to wing it. I could look back on certain of my own decisions and see them as guidelines, but I could never really have guessed the direction my decisions would take me. Truth is, I may have ended up at exactly the same level if I had done everything absolutely "right," but I don't think so.

I spoke to the diversity office at one point during my OCA days, the mid-nineties, and complained about the growth problem for women in the DO. The man that managed that group responded to me that the women in my career group, notably those of my CT class (90 men, 9-10 women) were above the average grade level for the entire group. I was somewhat taken aback until I heard the breakdown of the statistics. By this time, there were only two of us women left from the DO group of that original CT class, and a sizeable number of men. The two of us had GS-15 and 16 grades respectively, making the female average GS 15.5. The average for males was about GS-14, he said, as it was for retirement DO males overall. This was considered a good grade, but it covered a large number of males, including those who held all of the top positions in the Directorate.

By now the Clintons were in the White House, and for obvious reasons, women began to be taken seriously. Until now, who would have dreamed of a woman as attorney general? Much less in a foreign policy assignment, as Secretary of State? And the First Lady and Secretary of State were Wellesley women. How could I not like that? These appointments represented a sea change. At least that's how I saw it. Now women were beginning to be given jobs that had previously been done only by individuals with X and Y chromosomes. We were well past the days when a senior male would question whether a woman could understand "throw weight," a reference that had distinguished Ronald Reagan's chief of staff, Donald Regan, who said women preferred "human interest" stories. This kind of talk was ending. With the Clintons, I began to notice the movement of women into senior positions with real substance. It was remarkable. While I had seen some progress in the 1980s, I was now witnessing real, institutional change.

Halfway through my OCA tour, the DCI placed a woman as head of OCA. She was a youngish, talented intelligence officer from another service, and she already had her Senior Intelligence Service (SIS) grade, something that now looked obscenely remote for me. What surprised me was not only that she would become director of OCA, but that she was married and had a real family life with commitments and obligations. This was culture shock to me. It was hard enough to imagine a woman getting to a substantive senior position in the DO, but a married, feminine, and attractive woman seemed out of the question. It was thus somewhere in the early 1990s that

I began to see real change in the organization, though admittedly I was not sitting in the DO at the time.

But change was beginning to take place in the DO as well. This was helped in part by a major class action suit filed by a set of female case officers in the Directorate, officers who joined together to fight for lost promotions and increased opportunity. At one point I myself spoke with the attorneys handling the suit. My clandestine experience somewhat predated the exact parameters of the class filing the suit. Further, the attorneys indicated that they thought I had already done well. This was not to prevent me from joining, but was merely their observation that I was doing well among the women who were part of the suit.

I kept thinking about the suit and wondering about its potential outcome, though I had fairly temperate views about the whole thing. I had lunch one day with a senior male colleague I greatly respected and who had always hoped to see me progress in my career. We discussed the suit. He urged me not to become part of it, expressing his strong negative view about the women who were in the suit. I would not want to align myself with them, he said. Further, you are doing well. Why taint yourself with this?

My temporary absence from the DO, my meeting with the class action attorneys, and the words of this particular colleague all led me to a fairly agnostic position on the case, and I simply refocused on the considerable demands of OCA and pursued it no further.

In retrospect, the success of the suit proved to be a major step forward for women in the DO. Some financial and promotional rewards were made and select women began to move very quickly in their careers, women who were deserving, but who now saw promotions at a kind of Mach speed that I had not previously witnessed in my Directorate.

Still, moving women way up the ladder remained slow in the DO. I wish I could view with humor what I then began to hear about men's struggles with putting women in the most senior positions. Namely, that while the DO wanted to move women ahead, very few had the requisite management experience to go on to the more senior assignments. This is a sine qua non, since of course the opportunity had not been there! So, women were now being recognized, but none were really qualified for the top jobs because they lacked the experience. True. But for very good reasons. Opportunity for growth has been suppressed.

These changes became most clear under Clinton-appointee DCI's James Woolsey and John Deutsch. Deutsch clearly came to the CIA with an agenda. And at least one part of it was to break up the old boy network of the DO. He appointed a woman, Nora Slatkin, as executive director of the organization, arguably the number two or three position in the Agency. I viewed this all as political in spite of whatever skills they could bring to the table. But the ice was now broken, and women were really being seen in serious senior positions in the Agency. The fight was still on, but criticisms and rebellion against this direction became more quiet and less overt.

Amid all of this a very good friend and colleague of mine, Janine Brookner, a case officer of my age group and one who'd had actual ops jobs overseas, was being sued by the Agency for sexual harassment. Janine was now Chief of Station in a real overseas COS job. She'd been accused by an immediate subordinate. I can't imagine what horrific sexual thing she must have done, but she surely did not rape anyone or physically attack anyone as she was a petite woman who could not possibly have shoved a man against a wall.

In the end, the case was settled and she was given a payment, but knowing her career was now dead-ended, she decided to quit the Agency. This remarkable woman took the money she had been given and in midlife got a law degree. She became extremely accomplished in handling carefully selected whistle-blower cases, and in the end, just before her death, she was working on the Havana Syndrome, a cluster of what are referred to as idiopathic symptoms experienced mostly overseas by U.S. government officials and military personnel serving in select sites abroad, such as Havana. Her death was untimely. She was truly a successful female, a new role model at last.

CHAPTER TWENTY-THREE

OVERSEAS AT LAST

Luck suddenly turned my way. My old division—to whom I still "belonged" though "on loan" to OCA—asked me if I would like to take a new assignment—to Europe. As I had been ruminating about retirement, I was so unprepared for this question that my initial response was not particularly positive. After giving it some thought for the next two days, it became crystal clear that the only answer to this offer was yes. I quickly called my old office and expressed my deep interest in the assignment.

I would not have a management job in this new position. It was a lateral assignment, same grade, no promotion, but it was a plum job, one that would broaden my worldview and my whole career experience. As a wise younger man in my office said to me while I was pondering, "What do you want on your tombstone—'Diplomat in Europe' or 'Branch Chief in Headquarters'?" Somehow his words summed up the situation, and my decision was made! At long last I would go overseas.

The next few months were filled with the excitement of preparing and planning for this tour. I still had to pass the medical, psychological testing, and related administrative challenges, but they were part of the game. It was to be.

So I spent the last three years of my career in the most reward-ing assignment of my life in the CIA-overseas. Out of the manage-ment stream, I could concentrate once again on substance, and so I did. For the most part I sat back and watched the management deci-sions. Occasionally I would experience an outburst—when I heard a "new idea" that I had seen played a decade or two decades before, for example. It was like clothes coming back in style, but each time a new team would get credit for innovation. Bit by bit these stops and starts in fact moved the organization forward.

I had the good fortune of working now for a chief, in fact two, during my duration in Europe, both of whom I respected and liked. The first brought significant international experience, open-minded-ness, and professionalism to the job, and it was a delight to encoun-ter these all in one manager. But there would still be odd challenges.

On one occasion, when the DCI and DDCI came out to visit, I was encouraged by a manager to express some of my views about the layering and bureaucracy within the system. Somewhat reluc-tantly, but then with a bit of a push from the manager just under the COS, I commented on all of this within our organization. The senior officer accompanying the DCI was a military man, and one who I suspected was not used to the more open and direct behavior of CIA employees than the military he was used to dealing with. He looked at me and asked if I hadn't noticed a change within the last year. I immediately understood that he thought there had been significant delayering since he had joined the organization in a top management position. I saw the "party line" answer. There really wasn't much left to say at this point, since he thought the seniors had addressed this problem, and his eyes glazed over with disinterest at my remaining few remarks. By now, I knew when to keep my mouth shut.

I finished my Europe assignment shortly after the Russian economic crisis of August 1998. I had closely followed the markets and the state of the ruble. When I saw it and the Russian economy collapse in late 1998, I saw another chapter ending. The Cold War was over, and the Russians first solid attempt as an emerging market, as a capital player, had failed. Stories of corruption and setbacks in Russia were rife. Oligarchs were taking over major entities and becoming part of the new Russia. I knew it would be some time before we would see the emergence of that critical nation into an integrated world, or global economy.

Still, it was an exciting time, watching the former USSR develop into a new nation. I observed the absence of a defining U.S. policy toward Russia—and the challenges of making it—most of which I now believe was done in a sort of default way by the American private sector. I watched as the frequently drunk head of state Boris Yeltsin survived in spite of endless alcoholic episodes. And I left just before the emergence and presidency of one Vladimir Putin in 2000.

By mid-tour in Europe, I had to give serious consideration to my next steps. I had in fact become so involved again in my work that I was thinking about follow-up assignments in Washington or elsewhere abroad. But I had now put in thirty years and was in what would have to be viewed—though I had not initially seen it as such—as the final assignment of my career.

CHAPTER TWENTY-FOUR

TRANSITION—GOING "OUTSIDE"

The Agency gives one final and useful benefit to its departing employees, and that is the option to take what is referred to as a Transition Course. This is a brief period of training, held in the Washington area, that helps the long-term CIA operations officer prepare for life "outside." The course is well justified, largely because so many DO employees have worked undercover and carry so much sensitive/classified information in their heads. The counterintelligence issues alone legitimize the course, i.e., the need to be reminded of how much of what one knows is classified. The final training discusses issues that develop for the CIA employee when they leave—new jobs, résumés, negotiating a fee or salary, what to say about their past career, and how to continue contact where appropriate with the Agency.

I returned from Europe and headed directly to Washington for the course. I had forgotten how complex and demanding our CIA world is since I had been inside it so long. But on returning to DC to finish up and sign out, I had a few hints at the cutoff facing me. Upon arriving at the airport, I went to pick up the car to attend my training course. I had a lot of paperwork on me, but it did not include the name or phone number of the person who ordered the car for me. I thought the car would be there waiting for me—under my name. I could find no name and no record, and finally after a number of phone calls tracked down a "friend" who put me in touch with the right office and the signatory.

Uh-oh, contact within CIA would be even more difficult in the future. This was a tiny preview.

Finally at the wheel of my rental car, I headed, per prior agreement, to the locale of the transition course. I had a map, but it did not include the exact detail I needed, such as precisely how to get to the building and where to go when I got there. (GPS was not yet available.) In my business, many buildings and doors are not marked for easy identification. I determined the general area, but that was not enough. So once again, I went to the telephone and on an open line attempted via another "friend" to find out exactly where my training was being held.

I had barely returned and was already feeling unprofessional as well as somewhat irritated that I could not easily arrive, rent my car, attend my course, visit Headquarters, and leave. Bit by bit, I found it all. I guess the final blow was my missing badge. When I finally got to the right location, my badge had not been forwarded. Further, after some three years away, I did not recall my special, shall we say, pin number. I insisted that I was an employee and should be listed, but I could see that the guards were looking at me as if . . . Finally, I found a manager in my own division who recognized and vouched for me. And I was "inside" once again.

At the suggestion of a wise-guy friend, I chose to retire on Halloween 1999—Spooks' Night, just before the Millennium. That seemed propitious. But I could see that while I would retain my friends, I would lose the access I had become accustomed to over the past thirty-two-plus years. How would I feel when I could no longer enter the building at Langley, when I would turn over my badge and walk out the door for the last time?

That day came on October 31, 1999, and I handed in my badge with one sentimental request that they cut off the bottom and just leave it with me for my memories. But the guards said no and a polite goodbye. I drove off the compound and again wondered what it would be like to be in the "outside" world full time. Was there a life after the CIA?

I had chosen a perfect time to leave. I had had an excellent final tour. The obstacle course that I had faced through most of my career really was gone. And the Cold War was over. That is what I fought.

CHAPTER TWENTY-FIVE

BACK AGAIN

Times had changed dramatically over a relatively short period of history, some three decades. Under a new DCI from Capitol Hill, I felt that we had turned the corner of the Aldrich Ames treason agony—and of facing a post–Cold War intelligence world. Furthermore, women were truly beginning to be treated as equals professionally.

By the time I departed in late 1999, a female career officer was actually in charge of one of the four CIA directorates. And, in the DO itself, a woman headed an operational division. This had happened only once for a few months several years earlier, when a female case officer had been assigned as a division chief, but for health reasons, she was not in the assignment for long. Training and specifically the professional CT course that I had undergone some thirty years earlier now had classes that contained about 50 percent women. On top of it, they were going through the full training course, including the paramilitary/obstacle course training. In my old office alone, I saw that nearly half the professional staff consisted of women. All this was happening by the end of my career.

So much had changed historically, and so many good employees filled the CIA. I still thought we were heavily bureaucratized and layered. But the Cold War was over and, for me, with it the worst of national security concerns. At least, that's what I thought.

Still, I agreed with the new management line, attributed to former DCI James Woolsey, that the dragon may be slain but there are plenty of snakes and rodents to battle. The justification was that intelligence and specifically the CIA was as much needed then as it has been at any point in the past fifty-plus years. But the challenges were more abstruse than before, and everyone, especially leaders on Capitol Hill, were questioning the further need for human intelligence (HUMINT) collection. Why did we need so much funding for human reporting assets when the Cold War was over and the international threats diminished? Science and tech were the new heroes, and scientific developments became increasingly important—social media, cyber security, et al.

But cutting back our HUMINT budget came a bit too quickly, as we would soon learn.

Retired two years. Surely I wasn't going to go back? But 9/11 happened and everything changed. Suddenly there was a great cause again. No one could possibly accuse us of "mission creep" anymore. And Congress would have to approve sufficient budgets now—now that everyone else had finally recognized that we had a problem with international terrorism. We'd been focusing on it for many years and knew the dangers were out there all the time. The bombings in Eastern Africa in 1998 were blamed on a group called al Qaeda, little known to the outside world at the time. Most of us knew then that it was just a matter of time before something really awful happened. And it did on September 11, 2001.

My old colleagues had a position for me—part time and I wouldn't have to leave New York. That would be perfect. Part of the club again, earning some money, but staying away from Washington.

I got my papers in order and was ready to go back. It was the November after 9/11. Things were working out perfectly, and I could be involved again, in work that mattered. With plane tickets and hotel reservations in place, I thought I would make one more call to Headquarters before heading to the airport, just to confirm everything, since my badge would have to be ready or I couldn't get into the building.

Oh, good thing you called, said my new project manager. We just found out that you won't be starting tomorrow after all. Apparently your clearances need to be updated. But, I said, they were current and I had intentionally come back before they expired. He said they understood that, but now was a good time to update. I had, after all, been out in the "real world" for two years!

What about my tickets? I'd already paid for them, made arrangements for someone to take care of my dog and my apartment while I was gone. Oh, don't worry, he said, we'll reimburse you for all that when you're back.

Needless to say, I was irritated. What if I hadn't called? Would they have just told me to go home when I arrived? I reminded myself of why I was enjoying retirement—the substance of the job was compelling and exciting, but the bureaucracy! Oh, the bureaucracy, it can drag down even the strongest souls.

Maybe I should just stop now and continue in my new life, I thought. No. Oh no, the job was going to be interesting, and I needed to go back, with all this craziness going on around the world. There would never be enough trained people now to work on some of these projects.

But for now, I canceled my flight waited for the new security process to begin. Hopefully I would be back on contract within a month or so.

No such luck. For the next not one, not two, but four months, I waited to hear how my clearance was going and when I would begin. After all, the papers were pretty much in order. There wasn't much new information on me. I lived in New York, not Beirut, and I had increasingly fewer international contacts and travel. Nothing interesting to investigate about me.

Finally, I got the good news—well, the news—that I was invited to the "HQS area" for my polygraph.

Like everyone else I dread the polygraph, but I had been through it before and would just have to go through the process again. The last time I was in a good management job and had a great tester. He just had to tell me to breathe deeply when he asked my age. I wasn't going to lie about that; I just didn't want to discuss it. That poly went smoothly, and this one should as well, I thought.

So I made my reservations again and headed off to Washington.

I had sort of forgotten that you really have to have your logistics in place when you go back to the Headquarters area, much less when you are no longer an employee. I mean, first you have to know where you are going—the exact address and location of the "facility," with directions. Everything I needed was no longer at Langley, which is what I was used to. And of course I needed a telephone number for contact in case I got lost or was late. I had always discreetly kept phone numbers of office contacts and friends using my own codes, but realized that I no longer had that list or access.

I got to Reagan National, found my rental car, and headed out to the Virginia countryside to try to find the building where my test would be held. Finding new buildings is not my favorite activity, but I had good directions, and I worked my way successfully toward the suburban office where I would have my poly. It was beginning to look familiar, though I couldn't quite remember the exact location because it had been so many years since I'd had my last test. Ah, there it was—the street I need. But I couldn't find the exact address. Lots of buildings lacked numbers, and they all looked alike.

I had plenty of time, but I didn't want to be late for this appointment. After circling the area a few times, I realized that only one building had a security guard and assumed that this must be the place. The fact that the sign with the address was two digits off the number I had been given and was hanging upside down was mildly unsettling, but I thought I'd better drive up to the security guard and ask him before I circled once again and drew his attention.

The guard asked me who I was and why I was there. Sure enough, he said I was at the right place. He kindly explained that there was a problem with their address sign, and they expected to update it soon. Not very helpful since I had no phone number or name to contact and was using their exact directions. I reminded myself once again why I had retired. I was a little irritated, given that I did not have a map or any written directions from them.

So I parked and went into the building, where I immediately saw the security desk and guard. I gave my name and they were indeed expecting me, gave me a badge, and processed me through to the waiting area for the poly. I was in the right place! Only a few more hours and this final process would be over and I would be back in place, where I had expected to be months before.

The smell of coffee and popcorn wafted through the air, even though it was early morning. I recognized the fragrances and began to feel more at home. Near the elevator, I couldn't help but notice the printed "mission statement" taped to the wall. I had participated in so many mission statement–writing exercises. It was a favorite management activity during the 1990s, when we were being accused by Congress of post-Cold War "mission creep." In those days we did engage in a lot of management exercises taken from the best of the American business community.

By the 1990s, we knew we could benefit from adopting some of the skills of the successful core of the U.S. business world. This included writing mission statements, as well as "stepping outside the paradigm," having "walk-around management," "transparency," "buy-in" from nonmanagement, and review by your subordinates on how you were managing. We often called this "process". (I reminded myself again of why I had retired.) A lot of us felt that we spent too much time now on "process" and related meetings and should spend more time on substance and field activities, even if we were at Headquarters and couldn't be in the field ourselves.

Never mind, this was not my concern. I was here for my poly. I went into the waiting room for the poly candidates. I was the first one there. Not great, since I don't do well when I have time to sit and ruminate. Shortly the room filled with about two dozen people, to my surprise. I guess I thought I was one of two or three, but that was not the case. Well, I was just a redo, not a first-timer.

Eventually a young blond man came in to give us an overview of what we should expect. He introduced himself and explained that we would see a video that would describe the polygraph process. It was a standard video, one that repeated information that I well understood from previous tests, but I assumed it helped the newcomers feel comfortable. I couldn't help but notice that the young man doing the presentation was one of those "no shades of gray" people that seem to do so well in Security. I always wondered how these guys could know everything with such certitude.

I watched the video as if I were a first-timer. I am always overly conscientious and concerned that I might miss something important. In fact it was pretty standard fare, and I didn't learn anything new. I was pleased to hear that they continued "to update" the poly process and that efforts were being made to modernize and streamline this somewhat Dark Ages testing mechanism.

After the video, I sat and waited. Testers came in and chose most of those in the sitting room, but not me. I had been there the longest and wasn't getting called in. I began to feel like myself in third grade when I waited to be chosen for a sports team. I was always Team B. Finally there were only two of us left in the waiting room—nothing like "first come, first served."

The young blond guy reappeared, looked around the room at the two of us, one man, one woman, and said, "I guess I'll choose you," pointing to me. I accepted his offer and went off with him to the poly exam room. I wondered why he hadn't just introduced himself and said he would be my tester. That's normal, courteous business behavior.

We went to the poly room. I saw the familiar two-way window and the machine that would track my responses. The polygrapher asked me to sit down and explained that he would go over the questions with me before the test so that we could cover any issues that I might have. Fine.

We spent the next two hours talking about my London assignment, international travel, and my many foreign friends. I also observed that he had a big file on me on his desk. I guessed that that contained all my past contact and foreign travel information.

There was really nothing that I did in London, no foreigner I met, no foreign travel that I had taken that had not been properly reported by me. But it was several years later now, and I couldn't remember every trip to Paris, all the people I met, and so on, back then. I did think it sort of ironic that I was reporting on my own contacts and travel when that was already a matter of record in my file. I mean all that would be different now if I had forgotten somebody or some trip. And I knew I had been meticulous about recording every foreign meeting in foreign travel.

One of the parameters of the poly is that you just cover the period since your last test. That means that if my last test was ten years ago, my answers to the question should only apply from that date onward. Well, my mind doesn't work that way. If someone asks me, "Did you ever . . ." my brain doesn't date the answer. I knew this could be a little bit of a problem for me, but it was okay as I would just be giving more info than he wanted. Better than the other way around.

I'd forgotten how basic some of the questions are, such as "Have you ever committed a major crime?" "Are you, or have you ever been a member of a terrorist cell?" After 9/11, this was an understandable new question. I would have no problem with these questions.

After a total review, the polygrapher hooked me up to the machine, and we were ready to begin. It's sort of like an old EKG, where they attach wires and tabs to various parts of your upper body, but in this case to register your reactions, not just your heart. It does feel sort of strange to sit in a chair, with lots of wires attached to you, a polygrapher behind his desk, and a two-way darkened window in the room.

I didn't mind until he turned on the machine and I noticed that one arm looked normal, but the other one was bright pink. I hoped they knew what they were doing, since I wasn't twenty-five or even thirty-five anymore, and maybe this thing wasn't good for my body. He noticed that I seemed a little concerned and assured me that the body changes were perfectly normal. I did remember a friend telling me that she had sustained quite an ugly bruise after her poly.

Then the questions began. He repeated that I should just answer a simple "yes" or "no" to each of the questions, all of which we had now been over and which would recur in random order. Fine.

He started the machine and began with the first set of questions. "Have you committed a major crime in the past five years?

"No, I have never committed a major crime."

"Please, just answer with a simple yes or no," he repeated.

Oops, I overresponded. I needed to measure my responses but remain calm. Okay, that would be fine.

He continued, and I began my usual throat clearing, a sometimes habit caused by allergies. He stopped the questions and asked me not to clear my throat. That would be hard for me. OK, now I will try to measure my responses, breathe in, breathe out, answer a simple yes or no, and don't clear my throat. My arm was getting pinker, and I really had a frog in my throat now.

He had interjected a question as to whether I had "taken drugs" in the past five years, and I remembered that after I retired, I could try pot. I had been curious about it and thought I might try when I got to New York, where a friend of mine was an avid user. I told the polygrapher I thought I had tried it once but couldn't remember.

Two more hours passed, and he asked me if I wanted something to eat. I said that I would prefer to stay there and not take a lunch break until the test was done. Spotting the water on his desk, I added that I might like a drink of water. He said he would unplug me and take me to the water fountain. Well, I didn't want to be unplugged and start this thing all over, so I just said I would be fine. I was, of course, clearing my throat more and more, but I wanted to stay put.

After yet another round of the same questions, he said he would step out of the room to speak with his supervisor. I was very calm at this point but was anxious to get this finished. I didn't introduce an ounce of humor or anger, just staying dull and dry the whole time, but I was beginning to think of the smart crack responses I could make! They were buzzing through my brain.

He came back and said that I should go to lunch. I wasn't too happy with that decision, but got unplugged, handed in my badge, went to my rental car, and headed out to find the best northern Virginia fast food I could in the area. McDonald's looked like an old friend at this point.

After lunch, I headed back and we started the whole process over. I said to my polygrapher, "I guess I'm not doing too well," to which he replied harshly, "Why do you say that, just answer the questions." By now I knew the questions inside out, I said. He responded that they were random, so I wouldn't know what order they were coming in. Well, I was still anticipating them at this point, especially since I couldn't figure out what was wrong. I decided I must have failed to mention a foreigner I knew, but I had been over the slightest acquaintances.

We continued through this now unpleasant process. He excused himself again and said he was sending in his supervisor. She was a youngish African-American woman, who asked in a soothing voice what was wrong. I found her comforting, on the cool side of hot and cold interrogators. I said I just didn't know.

She responded very curtly, "You know exactly what you are doing. I am here to protect the national security of this nation."

What! Now I was getting both angry and offended, but still thinking I should show no emotion so I could get through this blasted test. I couldn't believe that this young woman, who wouldn't even have had a job if women like me hadn't paved the way, was suggesting that I was a threat to national security. It was laughable, but I didn't dare laugh.

My tester came back and said we would start again and that I should just "act normal." "Act normal." I hadn't heard that expression in years. All I was doing was sitting quietly and answering questions. I didn't even raise my voice.

I started to think that perhaps I should answer that I was involved in a terrorist cell or had committed a major crime of some sort. I began to see how lawyers in court could get a person to confess, and I wondered if in fact everyone was guilty of what they were accused. After a while, you just want to say anything to get through the questioning.

Another couple of hours of this and I was done. So was the workday and so was the tester. The bottom line is that he said he couldn't pass me. Now I was furious. I didn't even want to shake his hand goodbye, I was so offended. I think it was the uncertainty on the drug question that created the problem, but I couldn't really remember if I had taken a puff or whatever, so I couldn't answer with a "simple yes or no."

I'd had a three-decade career, worked my way along as an ops officer and then a manager, climbed up the steep ladder of female officers, contributed some outstanding intelligence, received awards upon my retirement, I didn't even travel much anymore, and these two people were suggesting I was a threat to national security.

I went back to New York and thought the whole thing over. I was rattled at the experience and couldn't believe I had agreed to go back after a successful career and a happy retirement. "Act normal" and "I'm here to protect the national security of this nation" kept rattling through my brain, offending me more with each repetition. Now I couldn't do the consulting and was thoroughly offended and irritated. How could I miss on the poly? There was just no there there.

I went out and found a new job and awaited my "adjudication" session in Washington, where they would review my case and determine if, based on my recent polygraph, I was too much of a risk to reinvestigate. This took another six weeks, by which time I told myself that I must be crazy to go back. The call finally came, and I went back down to the same building for my adjudication and repoly.

The adjudicator told me he did not know if I was lying or not, and then asked me the same questions over and over, but with no wires attached. He agreed that I could then be repolyed, and in came a more senior and experienced polygrapher, who explained the whole process to me. Once again. We retested, and by the end of the day I had passed my poly and was back on board.

All in all, the new job didn't last long. It was fine, but I felt the press of bureaucracy and a little too much oversight for the small assignment I now had. I had moved on and was starting to teach classes on the Cold War and espionage and was writing a spy novel on Russian poisonings. I continued my love-hate relationship with Russia, but now in the "outside" world.

EPILOGUE

It was a long ride, as you can see, but clearly the world and the CIA's Directorate of Operations began to change in the 1990s, adapting to a more modern era that involved professional women. The class action suit was a key player in that, but the times were as well.

The overarching message of my own career:

I did well for a woman of my era. I did well for a "girl".

THE INTELLIGENCE COMMUNITY

When the CIA was founded in 1947, there were only three other intelligence components of the U.S. government:

- The Office of Naval Intelligence (ONI)
- The Bureau of Intelligence and Research (INR)
- Coast Guard Intelligence

Today, the U.S. Intelligence Community is composed of the following nineteen organizations:

- Office of the Director of National Intelligence
- Central Intelligence Agency
- National Security Agency/Central Security Service
- Defense Intelligence Agency
- National Geospatial-Intelligence Agency
- National Reconnaissance Office
- Department of State
- Department of Defense
- Department of Justice
- Federal Bureau of Investigation
- Drug Enforcement Administration

- Department of Homeland Security

- Department of Treasury

- Department of Energy Office of Intelligence and Counterintelligence

- Army Intelligence

- Air Force Intelligence

- U.S. Navy, Naval Intelligence

- U.S. Marine Corps, Marine Corps Intelligence Activity

- Coast Guard Intelligence

ABBREVIATIONS

IC: Intelligence Community

DNI: Director of National Intelligence

CIA: Central Intelligence Agency

DO: Directorate of Operations, formerly Deputy Director of Plans (DDP)

DI: Directorate of Intelligence

STATION: CIA field office

COS: Chief of Station

CS: Clandestine Service

RUMINT: hallway rumor

HUMINT: human intelligence

ACKNOWLEDGEMENTS

I owe special thanks to Jane Cavolina, my wonderful editor, who had the great ability of getting me to "stop" when I came to the end of my tale. As most writers know, it is very hard to let go. And thanks to my great Wellesley friends Judy Shaffer, Judythe Roberts, Leslie Engle and Susan Dunn, and to my dear friends and family, Dianne Weston, Nancy Bracken Garson, Joanna Beacom, and Robert Ashton.